NATIVE AMERICAN DESIGNS

for QUILTING

Dr. Joyce Mori

American Quilter's Society

P. O. Box 3290 • Paducah, KY 42002-3290

Located in Paducah, Kentucky, the American Quilter's Society (AQS) is dedicated to promoting the accomplishments of today's quilters. Through its publications and events, AQS strives to honor today's quiltmakers and their work and to inspire future creativity and innovation in quiltmaking.

MANUSCRIPT EDITOR: BARBARA SMITH
BOOK DESIGN/ILLUSTRATIONS: CASSIE ENGLISH
COVER DESIGN: MICHAEL BUCKINGHAM

Library of Congress Cataloging-in-Publication Data

Mori, Joyce.
        Native American designs for quilting / by Joyce Mori.
                        p.   cm.
        ISBN 1-57432-710-0
        1. Quilting--Patterns. 2. Quilts--Themes, motifs. 3. Indian art--North America. I. Title.
TT835.M684   1998
746.46'041--dc21   98-27956
                                                             CIP

Printed in the U.S.A. by Image Graphics, Paducah, KY

Additional copies of this book may be ordered from the American Quilter's Society, PO Box 3290, Paducah, KY 42002-3290 @ $15.95. Add $2.00 for postage & handling.

CONTENTS

ACKNOWLEDGMENTS

Theresa Fleming of Aurora, Colorado, did a wonderful job converting my designs into patterns suitable for machine quilters. More and more quilters are realizing how artistic and useful quilting by machine can be.

My husband, John, deserves major thanks for always putting up with my quilting projects spread throughout several rooms in our house as well as the works in progress in our shared studio. He is my favorite judge and critic of my work.

INTRODUCTION

Welcome to the pages of *Native American Designs for Quilting*. The more than 150 designs, spanning from prehistoric to historic times, have been adapted from many Native American cultures. The motifs come from pottery, rugs, beadwork, silverwork, woodwork, etc. Where possible, the designs have been identified as to tribe or region. They are arranged by category, for example, small motifs, designs for specific shapes, patterns for borders, and whole-cloth designs. A section on machine quilting has been included and Theresa Fleming provided the expertise adapting the motifs into wonderful machine quilting designs.

This book has two main purposes. The first is to introduce you to the variety and beauty of Native American designs, and the second is to encourage your creativity. In each section, a series of elements are given that can be used as presented or manipulated and combined with other elements to produce new designs. I also give some strategies for doing this and show examples. Watch for the "Variation" boxes, which call your attention to ideas for changing the quilting motifs to make new designs.

The basic function of the quilting stitch is to hold the quilt sandwich (quilt top, batting, and backing) together. Not too many years ago when I started becoming serious about quilts, the actual quilting seemed boring and lacking in creative potential. I took several workshops on quilting techniques and on the designing and planning of quilting designs. As a result, I began to find that quilting was relaxing. As the process of quilting became more challenging, I began to really enjoy it. I have learned to accept that my level of quilting is not masterpiece quality, but it is acceptable to me.

Quilting is the last major step in the process of completing a quilt. It is the last chance to add more beauty or to reinforce a theme, so I hope you will look carefully at the designs and select at least one for your next quilt. I also hope you will have as much fun using these designs as I have had in finding them.

TRACING QUILTING DESIGNS ON FABRIC

The technique you use to transfer quilting patterns to fabric can vary with each project or design. If possible, I like to transfer the design to my quilt top before I baste the layers together. However, you do not want the design to wear off before you can quilt it, so you may want to transfer only a portion of the design as you go.

The type of marking device you use can influence when you mark the design. The advantage to transferring the design before you layer the quilt is that you do not have to make a quilting stencil from the design. Instead, you simply photocopy the design and use an *indelible* pen to connect all the dashes to make a dark, solid line. Place this copy over a light source and under your quilt top and just trace the design on the fabric.

If you are using this method with a complex design, I suggest copying the design onto freezer paper. Draw the design with a black *permanent* pen on the unwaxed side of the freezer paper. This step makes it easier to see the design through the fabric. Then iron the freezer paper on the wrong side of the quilt and trace the motif. The freezer paper keeps the fabric from shifting, especially when you have to trace many lines. I use a wash-out cloth marker for tracing, but use whatever marking pen or pencil you are comfortable with. I usually trace the design from the top to the bottom to keep my hands off previously traced areas.

In some cases, only one-fourth of a large design is provided because of the limitations of the page size. You will need to lift up and re-iron the freezer paper four times to complete the tracing of the entire design.

For designs that do not have much detail in the center, you can trace the outline of the motif onto clear plastic and cut it out. You can then use the cutout as a template for tracing the outer edges of the design on fabric. Even if the design has some interior lines, they can often be drawn in freehand just before you quilt the motif.

If you decide to make a quilting stencil for more complex designs, I recommend the hot stencil gun. It quickly and easily burns the channels needed. While this is more time consuming than just tracing a design, it is advisable if you are going to use the same design many times on a quilt. You can also loan the stencil to friends, and the design can become a permanent part of your stencil collection. I have also found that the leaded-glass pattern cutter with a double blade works well for cutting channels. I used the special template plastic recommended for use with the cutter and found the stencils easy to cut.

If you are using quilting stencils, you will need a device for marking in the channels. I usually use a wash-out marker or pencil. However, I have found the soapstone marker that fits into a pencil-like holder can be used also. I have also had success with a transfer or pounce pad filled with chalk powder. You wipe the pad over the quilting stencil, and the powder goes through the channels to mark the design. The lines made with the last two devices rub off easily, so you will want to mark each area only as you are getting ready to actually sit down and quilt it.

Workshop teachers and your own experience will lead you to select a method of transferring designs that works for you. Be willing to try new products on the market. I do not find that one procedure is superior to the others. The method I select depends on the specific design and the nature and the color of the fabric.

Always remember, you can reduce or enlarge the designs with a copy machine to make them fit your particular space.

SUGGESTED MATERIALS
light source for tracing • black permanent pen • freezer paper
• wash-out marker, pencil, or pounce pad • access to a photocopier

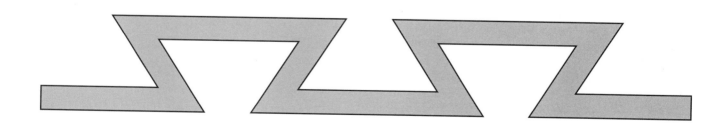

CREATIVITY WITH QUILTING DESIGNS

Altering the designs is not difficult and can be a lot of fun. Just study the illustrations to guide you through the process.

Take a sheet of paper and draw a line from top to bottom, approximately in the middle of the sheet. Then draw a line perpendicular to the first one across the center of the page, again approximately in the middle of the sheet. You will want to make at least 10 copies of the sheet. (Fig. 1)

Make four copies of a motif from this book. Cut out the motifs, leaving about ⅛" of paper around the outside edge. (Fig. 2)

Now, you can begin to manipulate this motif. A light box would be handy, but any source of backlight, such as a window or patio door, will do. Use tape to hold two opposite corners of the paper against the glass. Place a motif in each of the four quadrants in the different configurations illustrated in Figures 3–9.

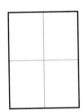

Figure 1

Figure 2
Birch bark design (Northeast woodlands)

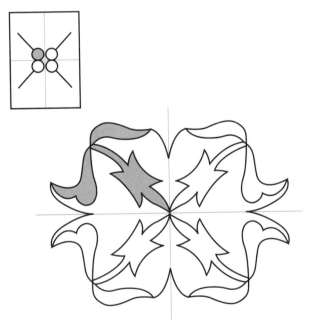

Figure 3 – Birch bark pattern 1
(Full-size pattern on page 13.)

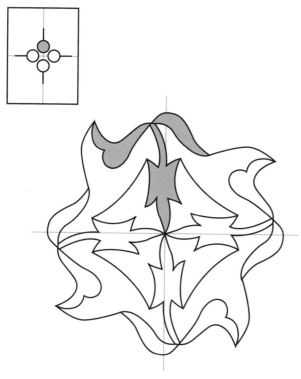

Figure 4 – Birch bark pattern 2
(Full-size pattern on page 13.)

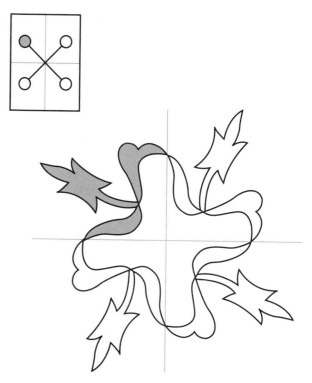

Figure 5 – Birch bark pattern 3
(Full-size pattern on page 14.)

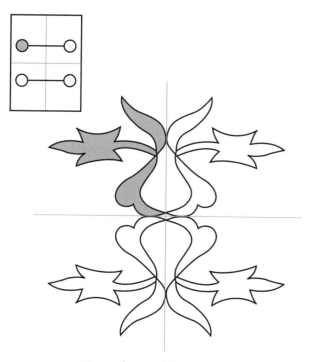

Figure 6 – Birch bark pattern 4
(Full-size pattern on page 14.)

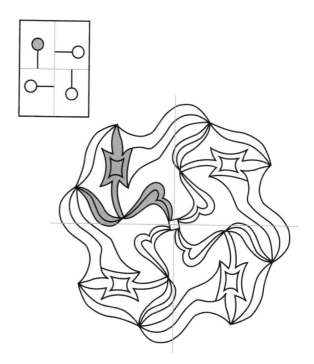

Figure 7 – Birch bark pattern 5
(Full-size pattern on page 15.)

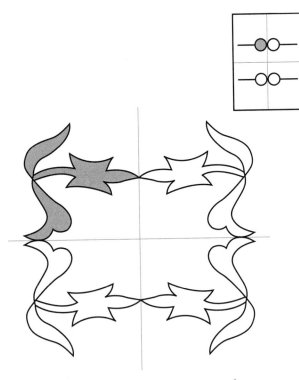

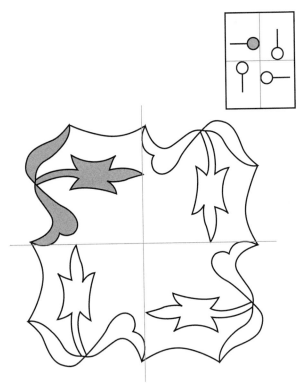

Figure 8 – Birch bark pattern 6
(Full-size pattern on page 16.)

Figure 9 – Birch bark pattern 7
(Full-size pattern on page 16.)

After you place the motifs in an arrangement, redraw the arrangement on a fresh piece of quadrant-marked paper if you like the design. Put all your new designs in a file folder. Even if you do not have a use for them at the moment, you may be able to use them in a future project.

You have just created new quilting motifs. That was certainly not difficult. Not all designs are pleasing in all arrangements, but a design can usually be manipulated in several ways to make new and attractive patterns.

You can often turn a design 90 degrees to create a more pleasing result. Figure 10 illustrates this idea. Look again at Figures 3 and 4. The motif was rotated 45 degrees until the design was oriented on the quadrant lines, which changes how the design appears. Extra connecting lines were added to both Figures 3 and 4.

The previous examples show a motif in a four-quadrant alignment. You can also try six- and eight-quadrant alignments. Many of the designs offer potential for further adaptations. You can enlarge or reduce your newly created designs on a copy machine. You can also enlarge or reduce a single motif before using it in new arrangements.

Once you have created a design you like, there are even more changes you can make. If you want the design to fill a smaller space, you can eliminate some lines or use only a portion of the design. (Fig. 11)

If you want the new design to fill a larger space, you have some easy options. You can enlarge the design with a copy machine. Changing the size of a design on a copy machine may take more than one try. Have a ruler with you so you can measure the design at each stage of reduction or enlargement. Don't enlarge your design too much. If you want it to fit a 10" block, make it about 9¼" across to avoid placing the design in the seam allowances. It is much easier to quilt through three layers (top, batting, and backing) than five layers (top, batting, backing, and two seam allowances). If you need to enlarge the design beyond the size of the paper, you may have to enlarge it in sections and tape them together.

Once the design has been enlarged, it may be fine the way it is, or it may have too much empty space to suit you. In the latter case, you will need to add lines, depending on how much actual quilting you want to do. Look at the birch bark pattern 5 on page 15. The motif was enlarged and extra lines were added to fill in the empty space. Some other points to consider: Are you using the quilting just to hold the layers of the quilt sandwich together? Do you want the quilting to reinforce the total quilt design or to be the main design in a whole-cloth quilt?

The more lines you add, the more you may lose the original design, which is generally not a problem. You have, in effect, created a new design. If it's important to you to keep the emphasis on the original design, you can quilt it with a thread that is a different color from the extra lines. You can also use outlining to help preserve the integrity of the original motif, adding an extra line of quilting about ⅛" to ¼" around the outside of the motif. (Fig. 12)

There are some other creative options you can try with individual motifs, as demonstrated in Figures 13 and 14. What would happen if part of the birch bark design were cut away? Could it be used that way? Perhaps parts of the motif can be made to fit into a triangular

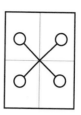
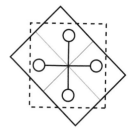

Figure 10

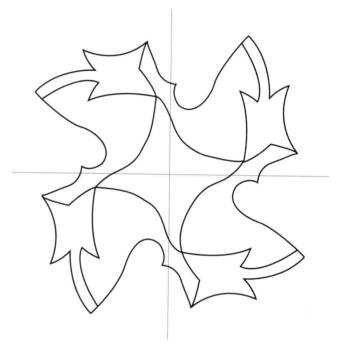

Figure 11

Figure 12

rather than square shape. (Fig. 15) Can the design be separated into parts? If so, perhaps one of the parts could be enlarged, another one could be reduced, and the unit could then be put back together again. Be open to trying different design options. Don't be discouraged if every variation does not look great. Experiment and enjoy yourself while you are doing it.

Figure 13

Figure 14

Figure 15

Native American Designs for Quilting – Dr. Joyce Mori

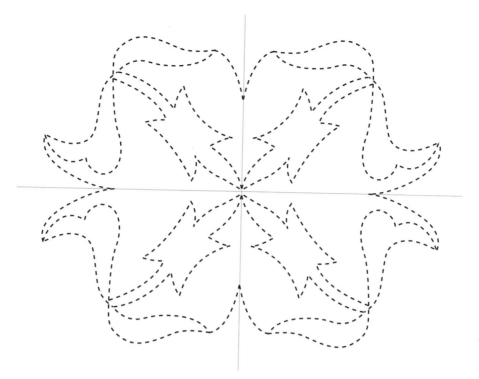

Birch bark pattern 1

Birch bark pattern 2

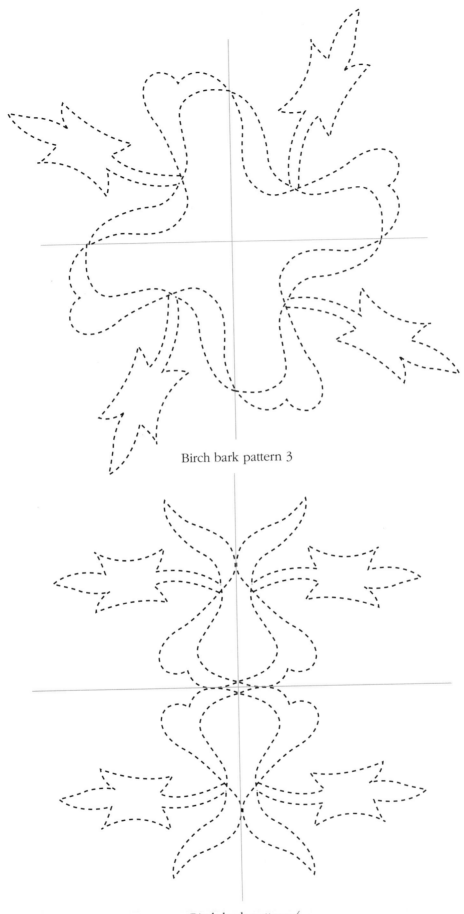

Birch bark pattern 3

Birch bark pattern 4

Native American Designs for Quilting – Dr. Joyce Mori

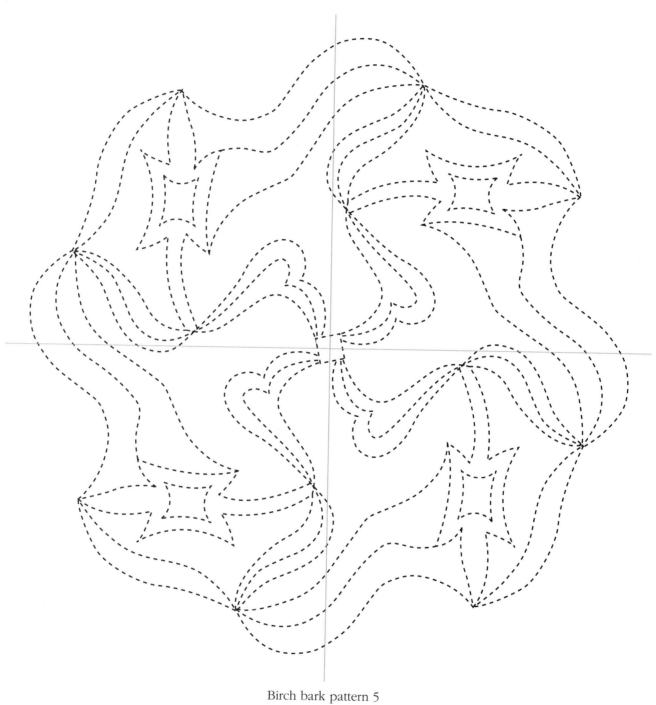

Birch bark pattern 5

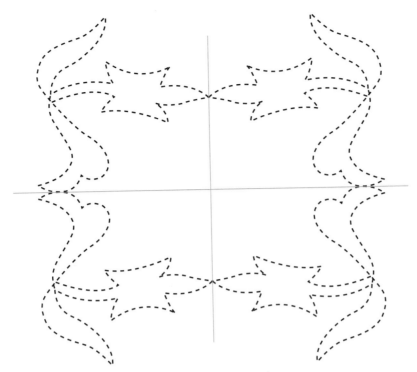

Birch bark pattern 6

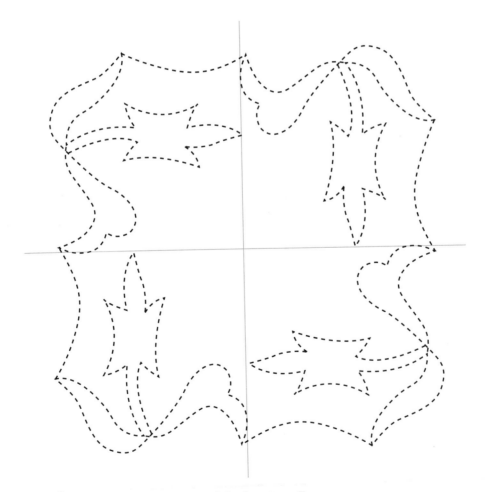

Birch bark pattern 7

Native American motifs make unique quilting designs, but they can also be used in wearable art and craft projects. There are other ways to use them in your quilts, too.

• QUILT LABELS

Don't you love to see an original label on the back of a quilt? Some of the Native American motifs make wonderful label designs. Look for a design that has space in its center for text; sometimes you can remove the center lines to create an open area for writing. Several quilt label designs are shown on pages 18–20. The quilt labels can be colored with fabric paints or colored pens.

• EMBROIDERY

Some of the designs in this book can be embroidered on a piece of fabric, and these pieces can be combined to create a quilt. The designs can also be embroidered on items such as Christmas stockings, place mats, aprons, etc.

• TRADITIONAL OR CELTIC APPLIQUÉ

Many of the floral or animal designs can be converted into appliqué patterns. Remember to enlarge them if necessary to eliminate tiny pieces. Some designs can be outlined with Celtic bias strips.

• HAWAIIAN-STYLE APPLIQUÉ

Start with simple designs for this application. Fold a piece of paper into fourths and place the design along the folds. Trace the design onto the paper and cut it out to make a simple Native American design in Hawaiian appliqué style. Fusible web and sueded fabric make this an easy project.

• FABRIC CRAYONS

Children can use fabric crayons to color a quilting motif outline. Draw a motif onto a piece of fabric that has been stabilized with freezer paper. This is a good way to encourage children to make their own quilts. Children in particular seem to enjoy the animal and people motifs.

Cree Quill Work

Variation

Subtract some lines
or an entire part
of a design.

Southwestern Silver Work

Hopi Wicker Basket Tray

Pima Basket

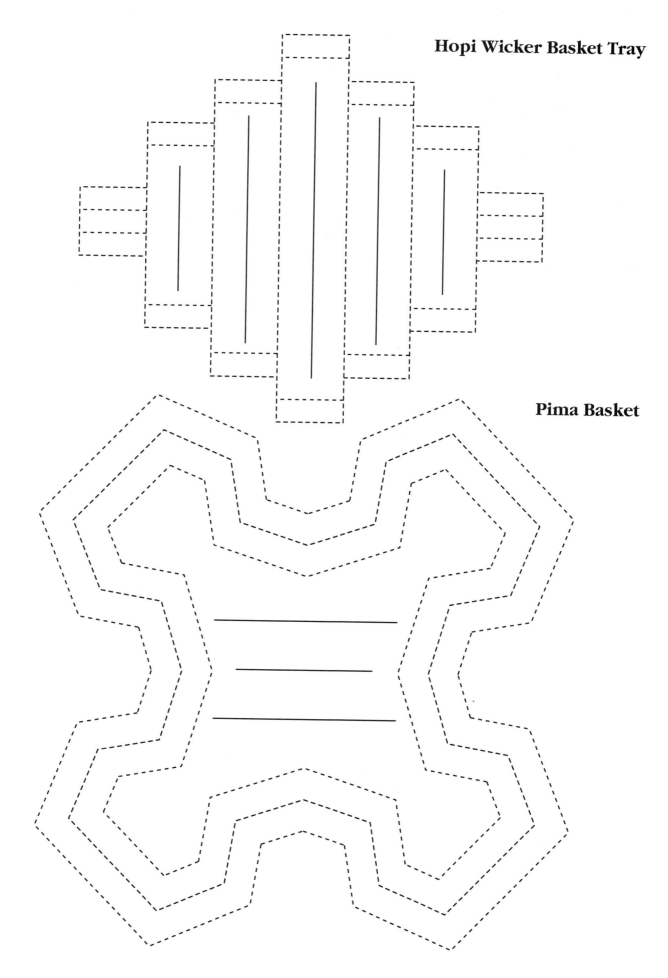

Plains Bead Work

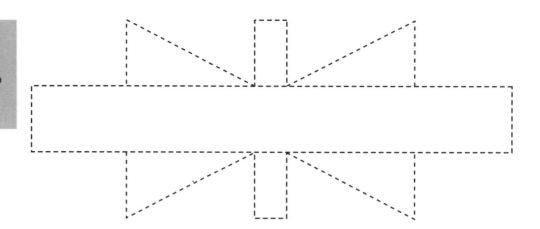

Navajo Silver Work

Many quilters enjoy making miniature quilts, so you will find some designs created just for small spaces. Some of these motifs can also be enlarged on a copy machine to fit larger areas, if you like. And, of course, some of the larger designs found throughout this book can be reduced in size so they will fit into smaller spaces. Remember, creativity is the key word. If you find a design you like, try working with it. You will probably be successful in making it fit the space you have.

As you look at the following designs, notice the single motif from which other motifs have been created. Often, this motif can be used alone, but it can also be manipulated into other configurations or combined with other motifs. I have provided some examples, and I encourage you to explore other possibilities. Sometimes only small changes are needed to create a design that looks great. I hope that providing you with these before-and-after motifs will show you how easy it is to vary the designs.

Northwest Coast Paddle

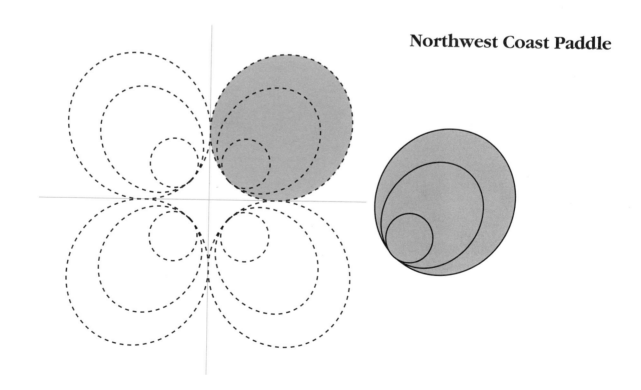

Eskimo Knife

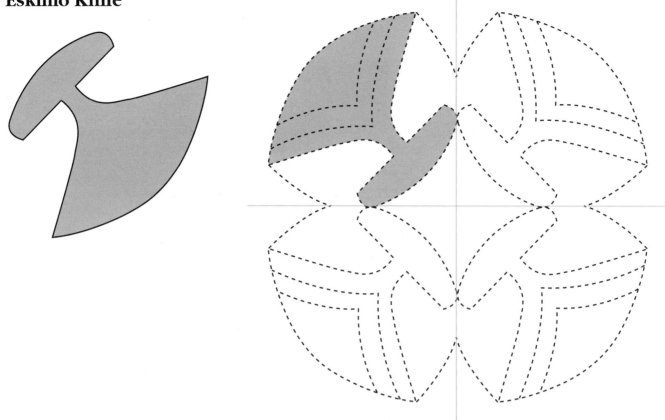

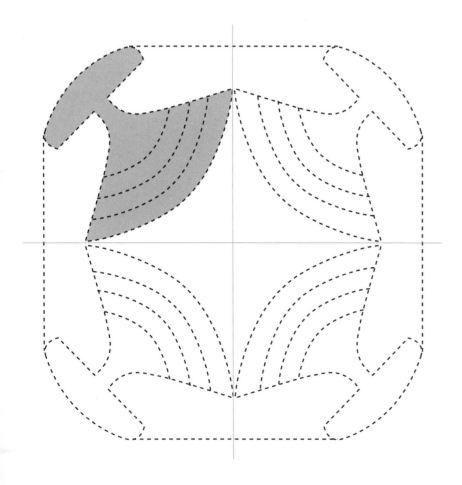

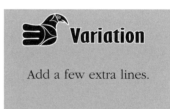

Add a few extra lines.

Northwest Coast

Acoma Pottery (Southwest)

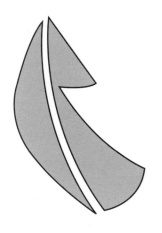

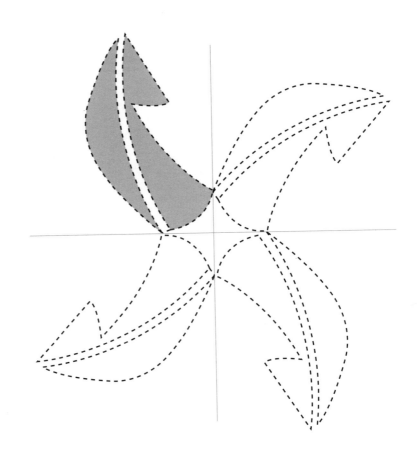

Navajo Rug (Southwest)

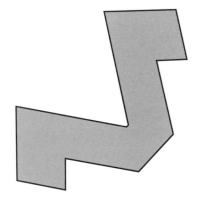

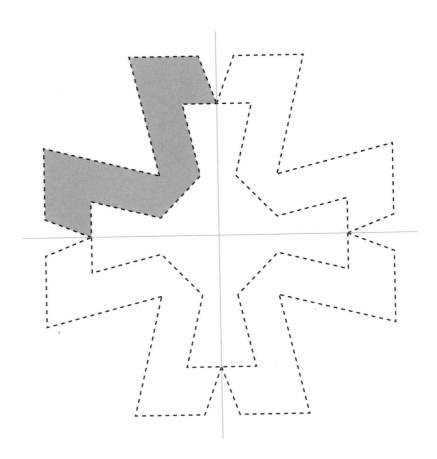

Native American Designs for Quilting – Dr. Joyce Mori

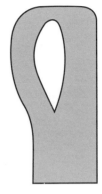

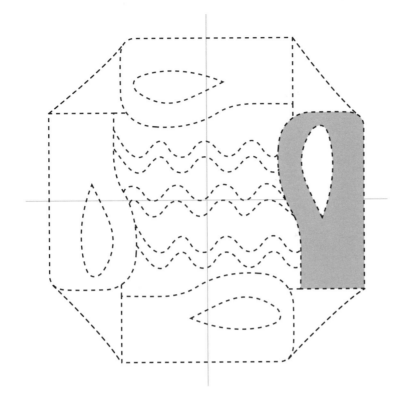

Southwest Weaving

Zuni Pottery (Southwest)

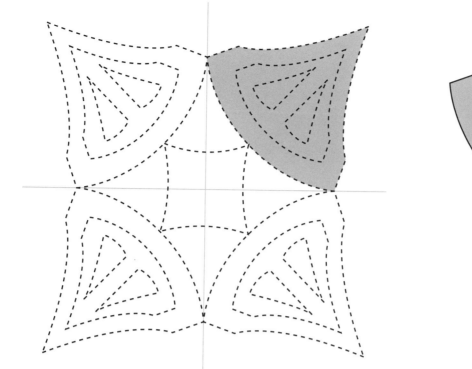

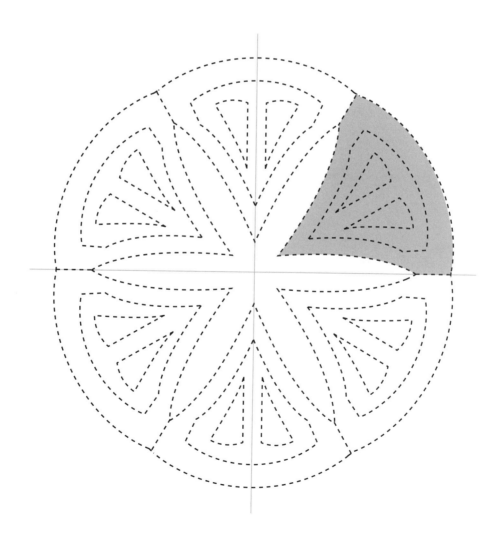

Hopi Basket (Southwest)

Northwest Coast Drum

Southwest Pottery

Variation

Combine two motifs and add extra lines.

Native American Designs for Quilting – Dr. Joyce Mori

Southwest Pottery

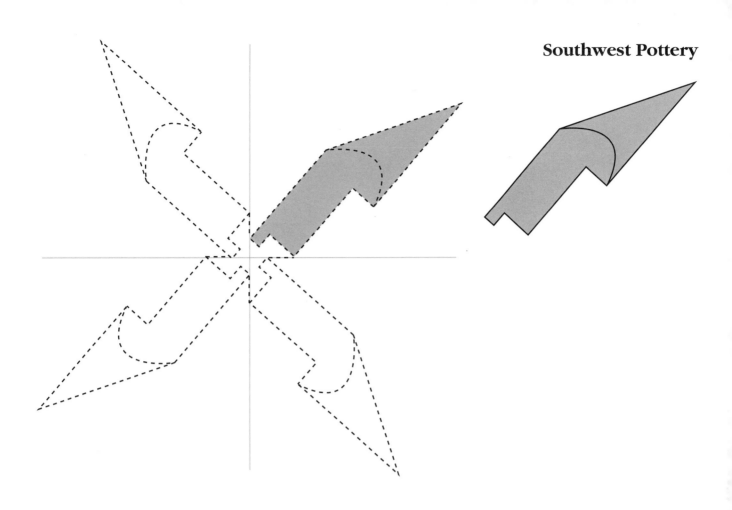

Northwest Woodlands Bead Work

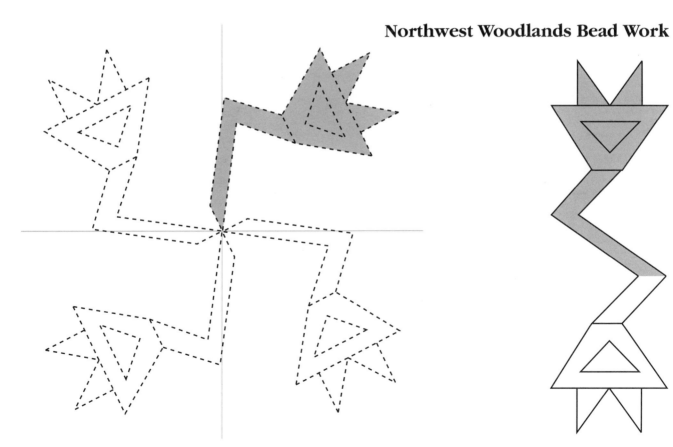

Cree Beadwork

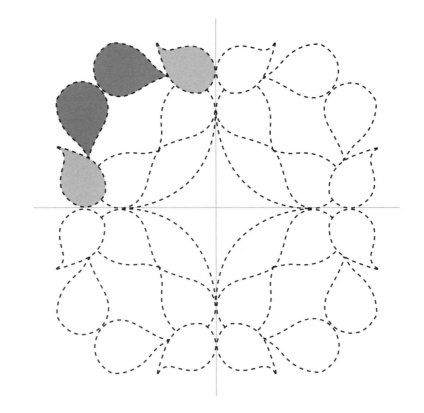

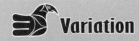 **Variation**

Use only parts
of the motif and
add extra lines.

Pima Basket

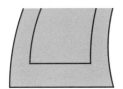

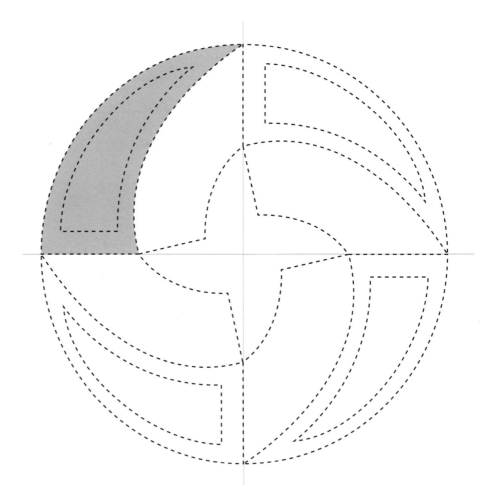

 **Variation**

Extend motif lines.

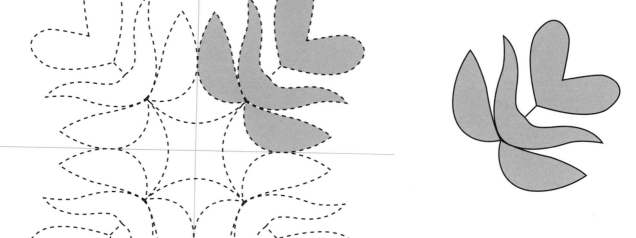

Cree Quillwork

Hopi Basket

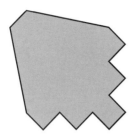

Variation

Use the interior design by itself.

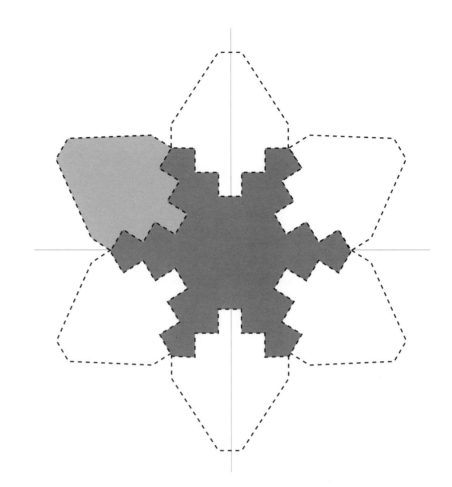

Variation

Use only part of a motif and add lines.

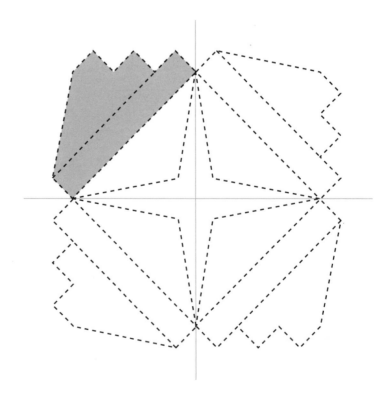

The designs in this section were made by combining several elements and adding extra lines or shapes to create a pleasing flow from motif to motif. In some cases, I have illustrated the original motifs. Other times, there was insufficient space to allow this, but you should be able to distinguish the separate units.

Because of space considerations, the designs are presented in reduced sizes. They can be enlarged to approximately 24" x 24". You may choose to add some additional lines, or you can keep adding new elements or repeats of the same elements to increase the size even further.

If you use the designs smaller than 24" x 24", you may need to delete some lines or elements. Whatever size you decide on, work with only one quarter of the design at a time. Draw the design on a piece of freezer paper with a permanent black marker. You may need to glue or tape pieces of freezer paper together to make a piece large enough.

Fold your quilt top in half and press the fold. Fold it in half again and press. The folds mark the four quadrants for drawing your design. The exact center of the top can be marked with a wash-out pencil to give you an additional reference point for aligning the design.

Iron the freezer paper to the wrong side of your quilt top and draw the design on the fabric with a wash-out marker or pencil of your choice. The freezer paper will stabilize the fabric while you transfer the pattern. When you have finished one quarter of the design, remove the freezer paper and place it in the second quadrant. Iron it to the fabric and trace the design. Repeat this procedure until you have transferred the entire design to the quilt top.

I think you will find it is fun and challenging to create and quilt your own whole-cloth designs. You will see how easy it is to combine motifs to create a large overall pattern.

Design in center of page is from Northeast Beadwork.

Expanding Star
Whole-cloth Pattern

Hopi Basket

Southwest Pottery

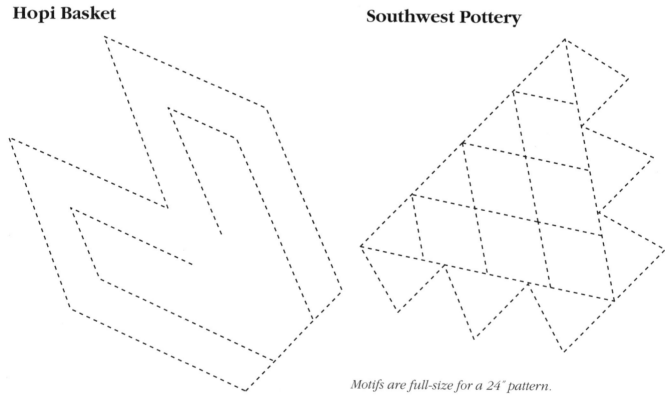

Motifs are full-size for a 24" pattern.

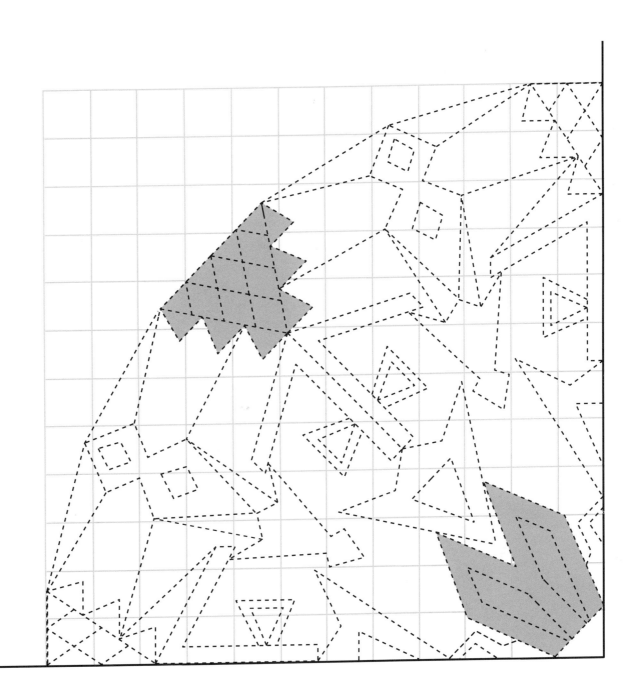

To enlarge the design, you can use the grid method
(1 grid square = 1″) or photocopy at 200%.

Native American Snowflake
Whole-cloth Pattern

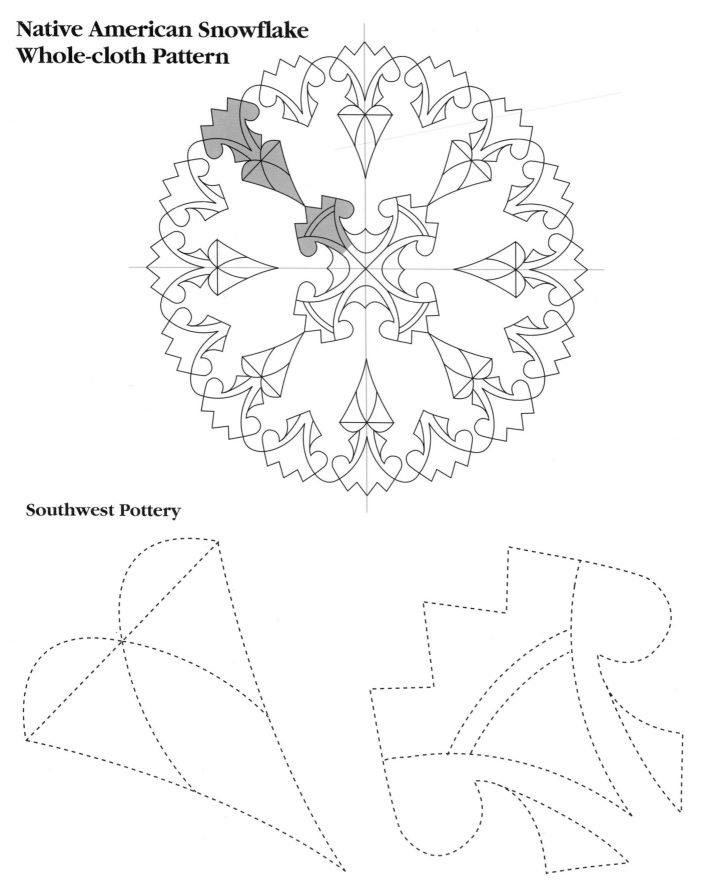

Southwest Pottery

Motifs are full-size for a 24″ pattern.

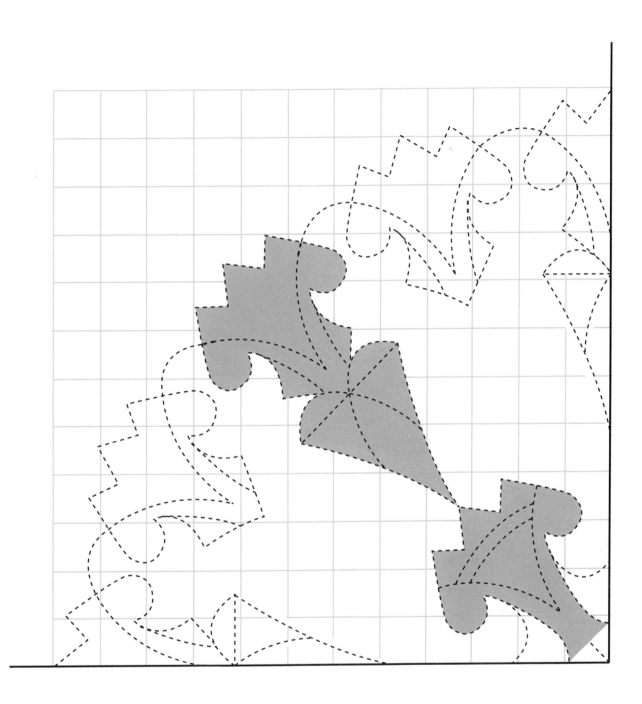

*To enlarge the design, you can use the grid method
(1 grid square = 1″) or photocopy at 200%.*

The Four Directions
Whole-cloth Pattern

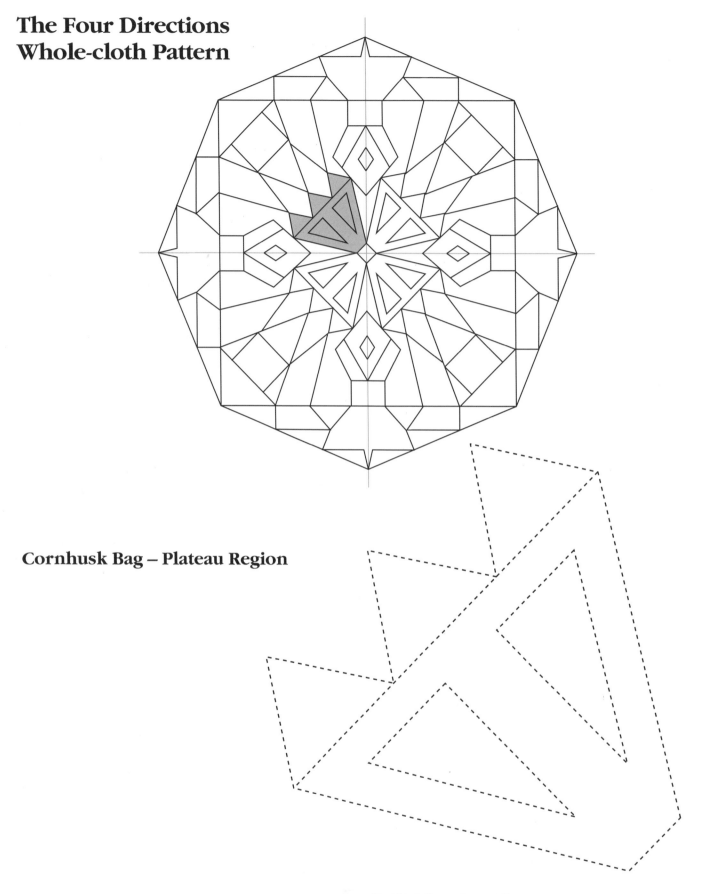

Cornhusk Bag – Plateau Region

Motif is full size for a 24" pattern.

Native American Designs for Quilting – Dr. Joyce Mori

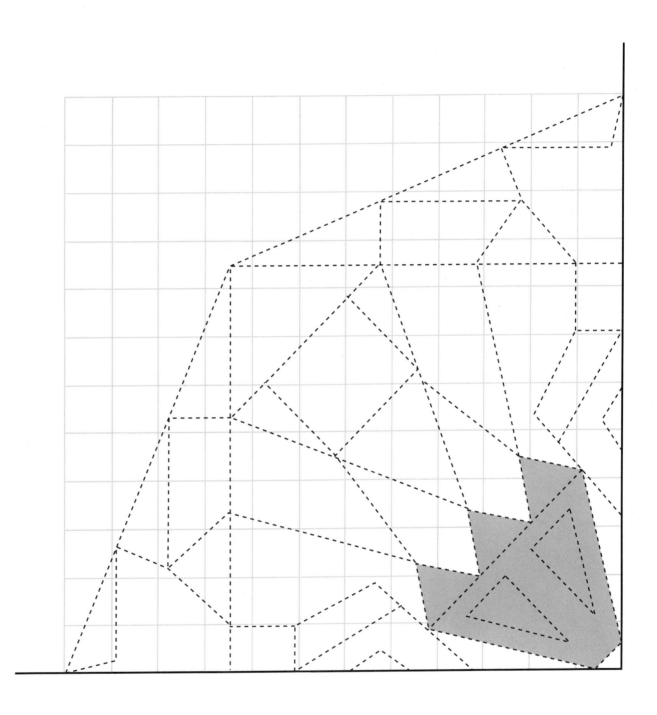

To enlarge the design, you can use the grid method
(1 grid square = 1˝) or photocopy at 200%.

DESIGNS FOR SPECIFIC GEOMETRIC SHAPES

The designs in this section fit into specific geometric shapes, such as right-angle triangles, equilateral triangles, squares, rectangles, etc. Other designs throughout this book may also fit such shapes, and some designs can be adapted to fit a needed space.

Crow Parfleche

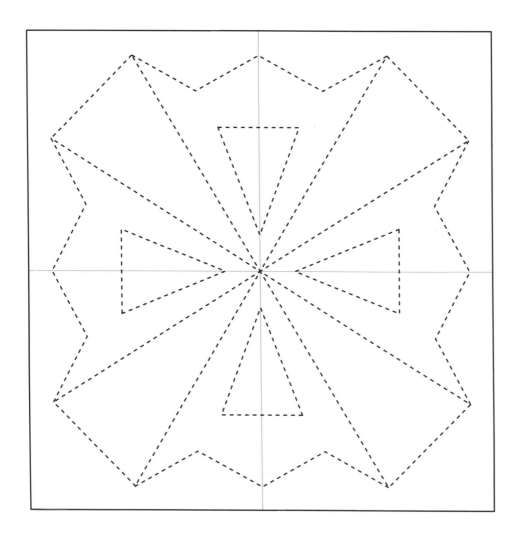

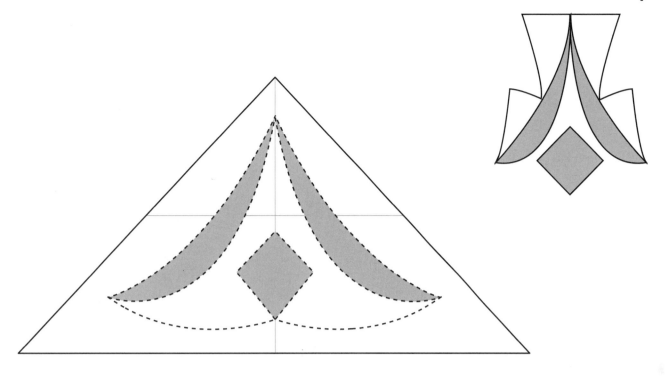

 **Variation**
Use parts of the
design and add lines
or other elements.

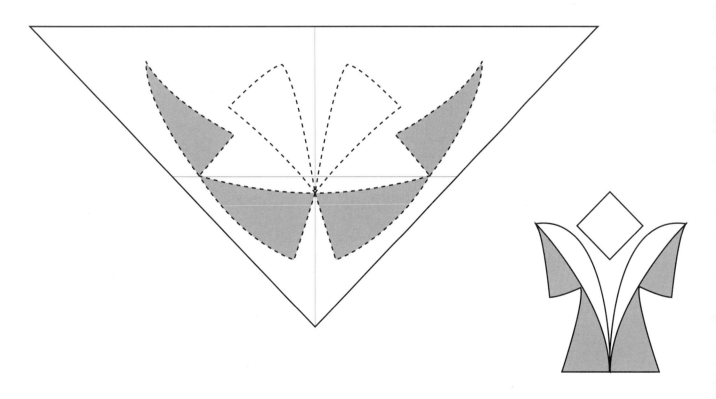

Hopi Basket

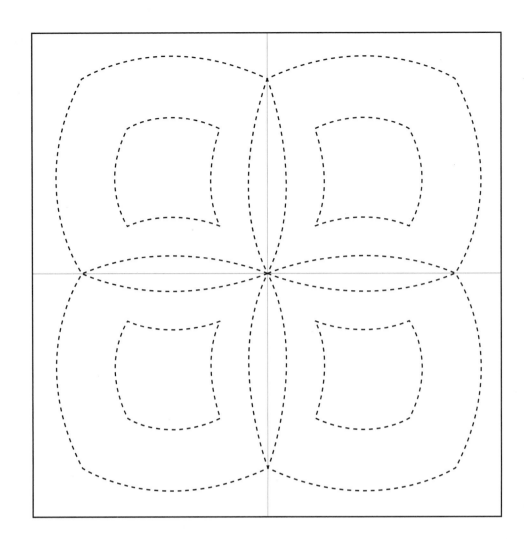

Osage Cradleboard

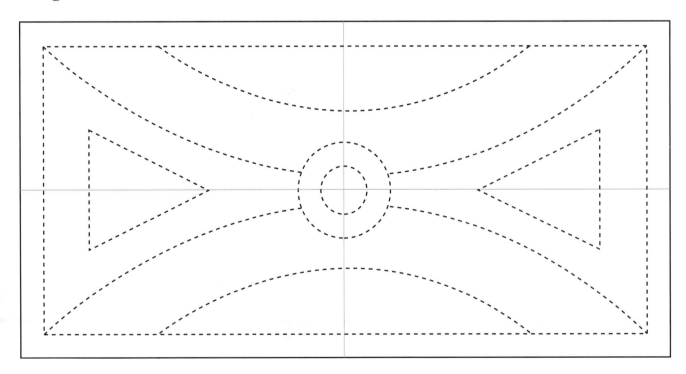

Native American Designs for Quilting – Dr. Joyce Mori

Zuni Pottery

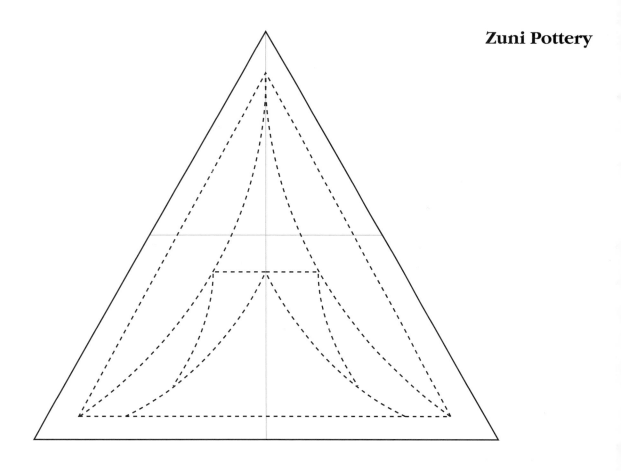

Navajo Rug

Cochiti Pottery

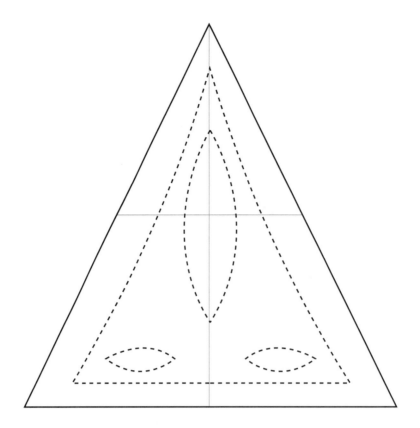

Acoma Pottery

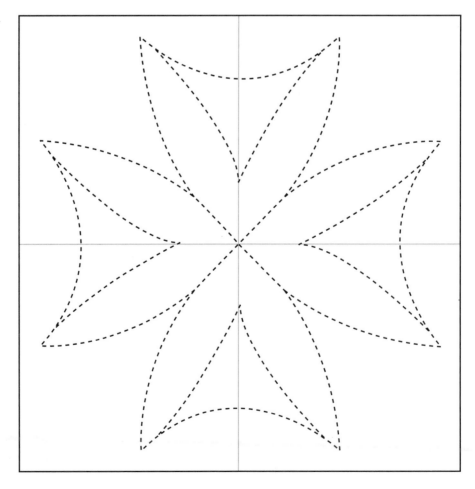

Native American Designs for Quilting – Dr. Joyce Mori

BORDERS AND BORDER CORNERS

Native American designs can be used to make wonderful border quilting patterns. In some cases, a portion of the border pattern is shown. However, to maximize the number of designs presented, some of the motifs are presented as single units, and you will need to create the border and the border corner from a motif.

It is easy to create borders and border corners. Study the border design on page 47. This border was created from the same Birch Bark motif that was used in so many different ways on pages 8–10. Remember, the border designs can be resized using a copy machine.

Southwest Woven Sash

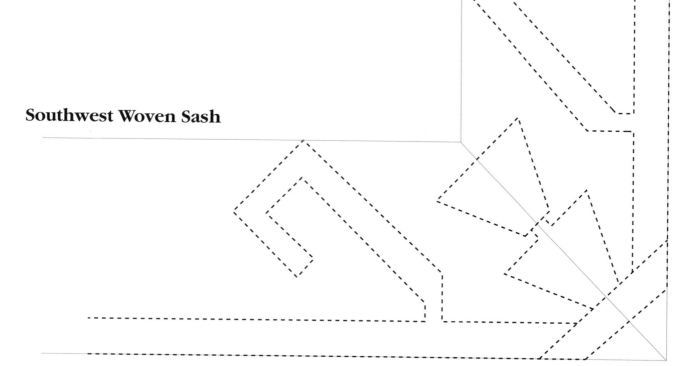

Midwest Woven Bag

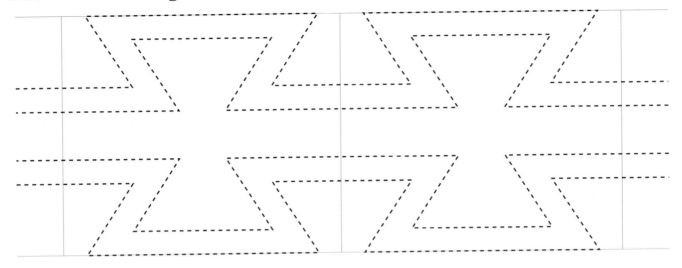

Combination of motifs

Southwest Weaving

Native American Designs for Quilting – Dr. Joyce Mori

Birch Bark Design – Northeast Woodlands

Southwest Pottery

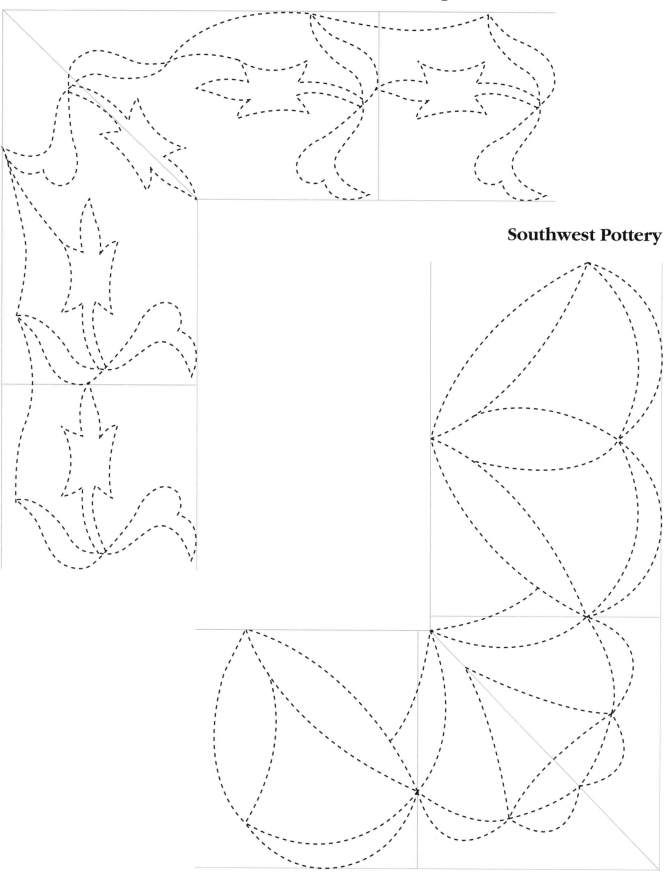

Navajo Rug

Navajo

Southwest Pottery

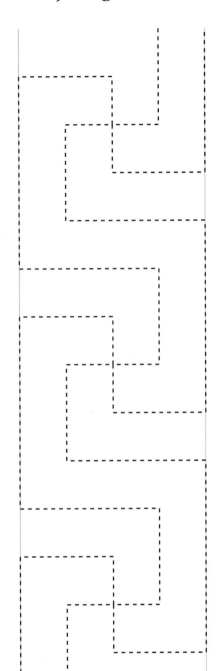

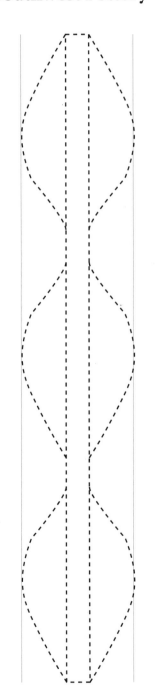

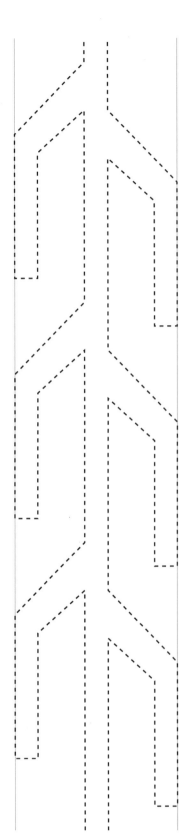

DESIGNS FOR MACHINE QUILTERS

More and more quilters are machine quilting, either with their regular sewing machines or with a hand-guided commercial quilting machine. I wanted to include some machine quilting designs in this book, so I asked Theresa Fleming of Aurora, Colorado, to convert some of my Native American motifs. Theresa specializes in continuous-line or edge-to-edge quilting. She calls it "texturing." The resulting designs can also be used to turn corners or to quilt within a block with hand quilting. We have provided recommendations for size, but you may need to enlarge or reduce the designs, depending on your quilt top.

Theresa enjoys the design and piecing aspects of quilting the most, and by using a commercial quilting machine, she can finish her quilts much faster than if she hand quilted them. She has her sketch book full of designs to sew, and machine quilting enables her to move on to her new ideas. She likes her commercial machine because it puts less physical strain on her hands, arms, and shoulders than her home sewing machine would. A quilter must coordinate her entire body to use a commercial machine. Theresa calls it "quilt dancing," and she turns on some good music as she dances her way across the quilt top.

Theresa selects her machine designs with the same criteria as a hand quilter:

- A complex design usually needs a simple quilting design.
- The name of the quilt or block might suggest a coordinating quilting design.
- The personality of the quilt owner can influence the choice of a motif. For example, ice cream cones would be appropriate for a child's quilt.
- Perhaps a fabric in the quilt top could suggest a design. A floral print might need a floral or curvilinear quilting design.

Generally, individual motifs are shown. In some examples, the design is illustrated with a variation. Notice that the lines in the motifs can be offset, used as mirror images, or sewn in parallel rows. Follow the direction of the arrows when you sew.

Theresa and I hope you will try some of these machine quilting designs; you might want to try your hand at adapting other designs in this book to machine quilting.

Delaware Beadwork

Start

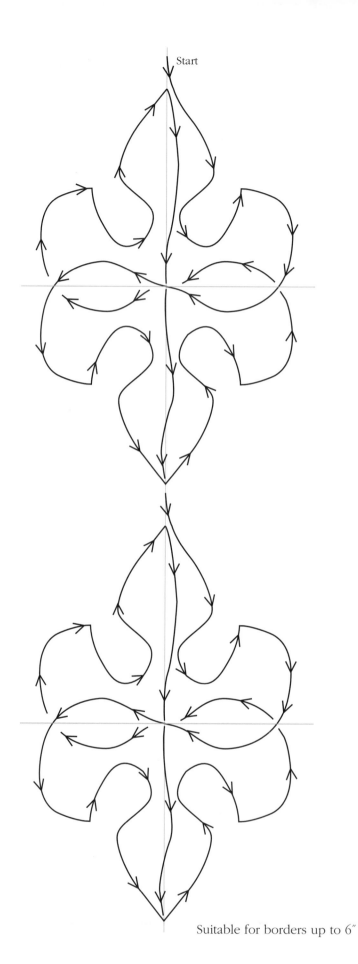

Suitable for borders up to 6″

Native American Designs for Quilting – Joyce Mori

Start

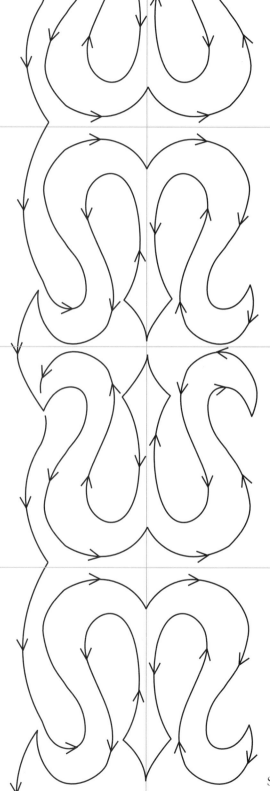

Suitable for borders up to 5.25″

Southwest Pottery

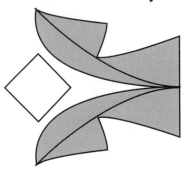

Start

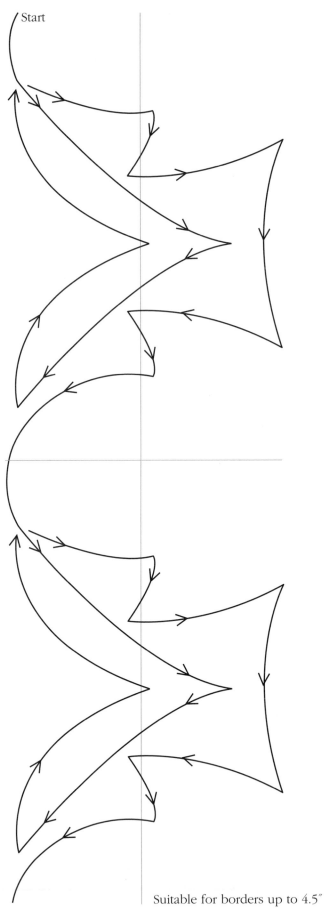

Suitable for borders up to 4.5″

Native American Designs for Quilting – Joyce Mori

Start

Acoma Pottery

Suitable for borders up to 5.25″

Northeast Woodland Beadwork

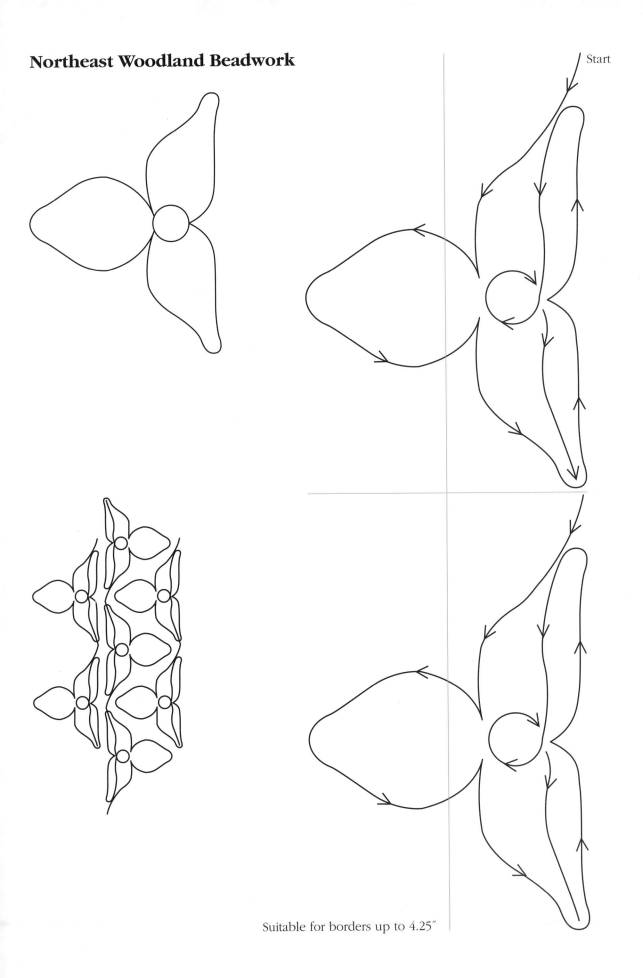

Start

Suitable for borders up to 4.25″

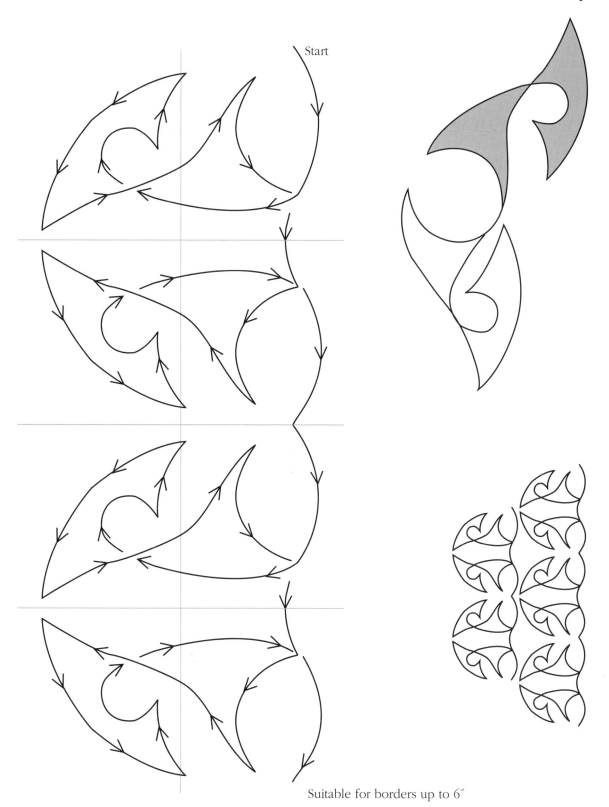

Acoma Pottery

Start

Suitable for borders up to 6″

ETHNIC DESIGNS

Quilters sometimes want designs that look Native American. Perhaps they want to reinforce the theme of a quilt or even to create a theme. The motifs in this section look like Native American designs. They were adapted for quilting with few modifications so that they retain their true heritage. I hope you will have occasion to use these designs in your quilts, and I think you will agree they are unique and attractive.

Prehistoric Southwest Pottery

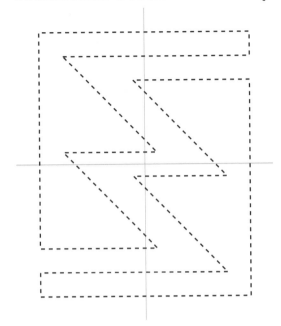

Plains Parfleche

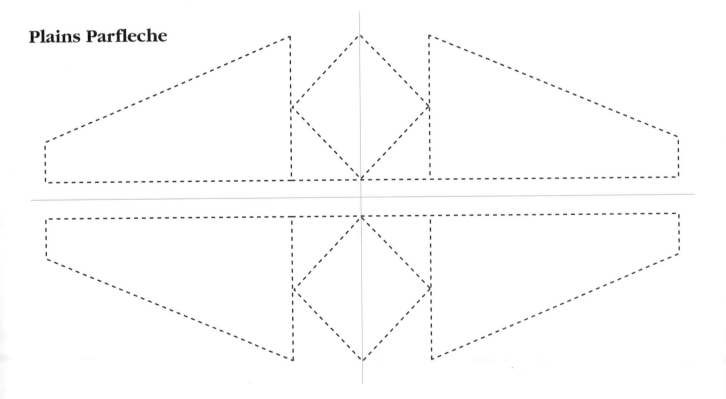

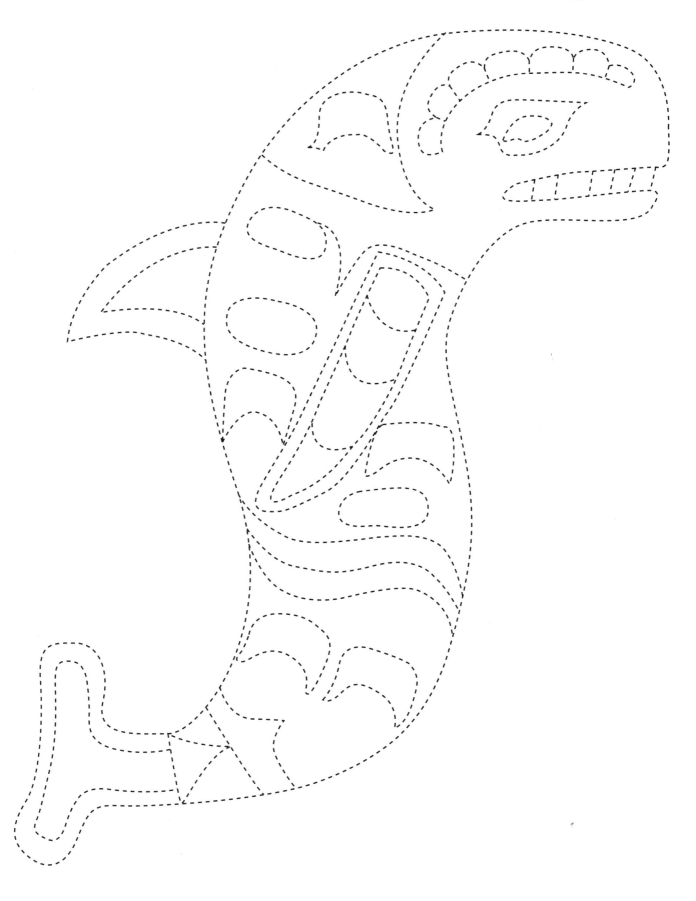

Northeast Woodland Beadwork

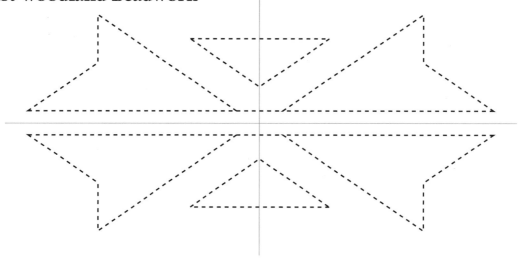

Southwest Wooden Tablita

Navajo Rug

Navajo Rug

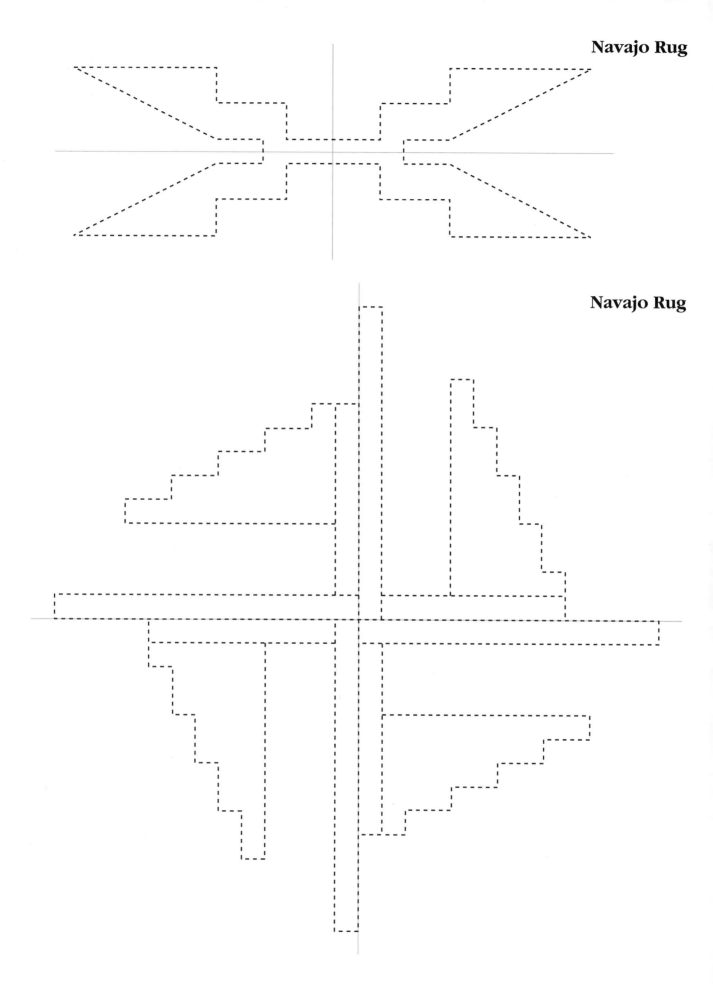

Northwest Coast Hat

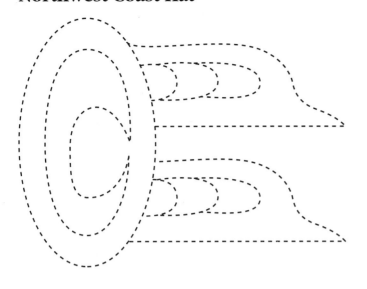

Southwest Pottery

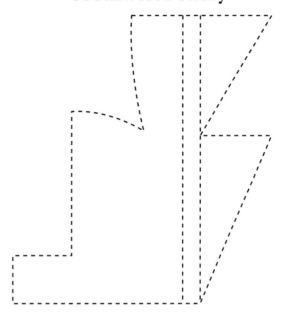

Hopi Wicker Basket

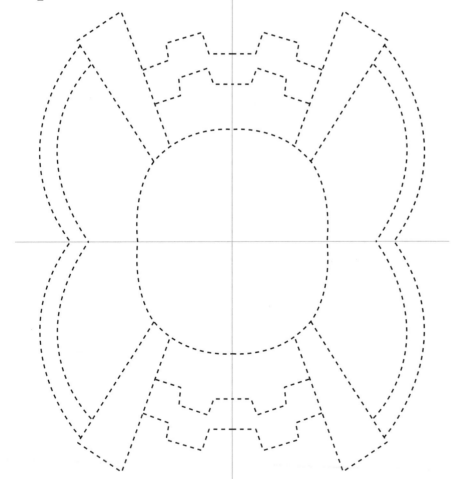

Hopi Pottery

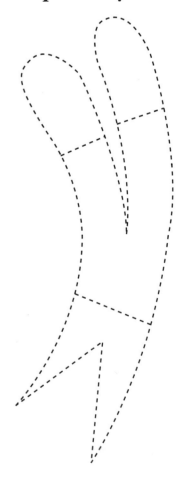

Plains Beadwork

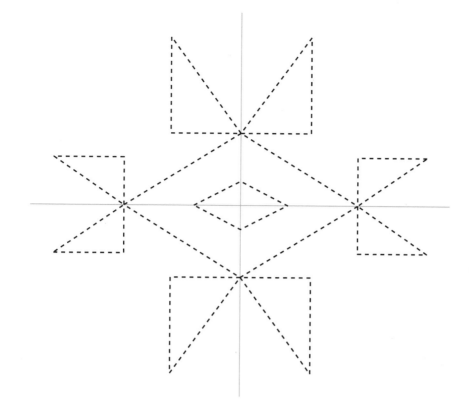

Southwest Basket

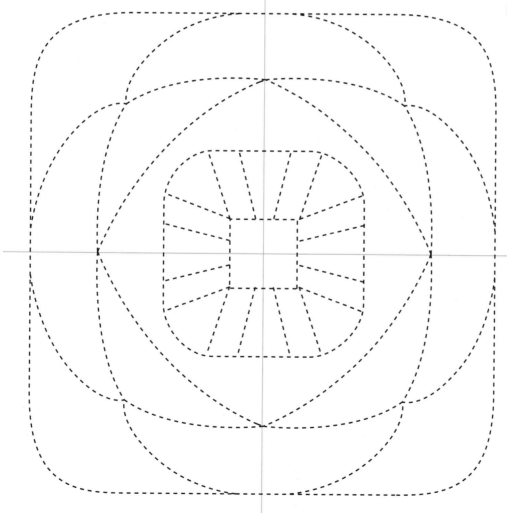

Northwest Coast (Cowichan) Spindle Whorl

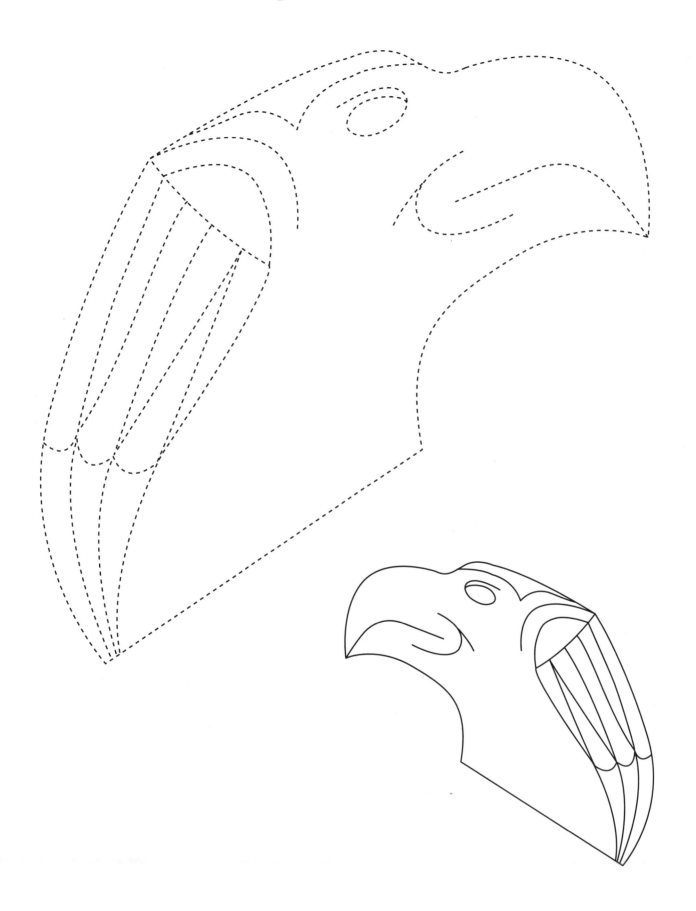

Southwest Corn Maid

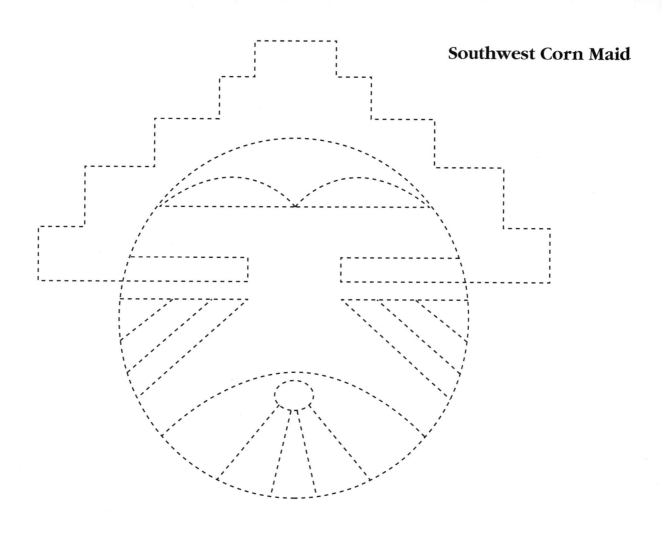

Southwest Pottery

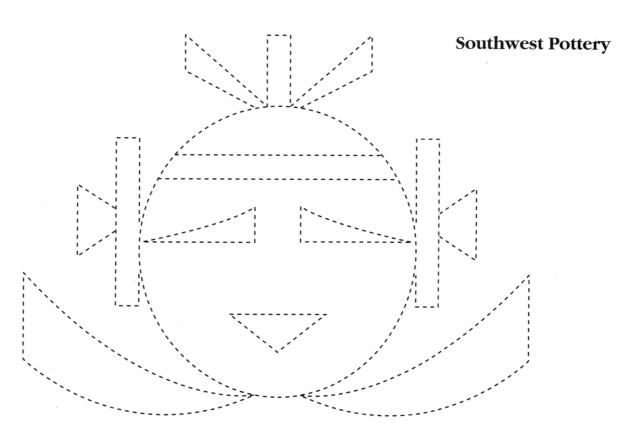

Santo Domingo Bird

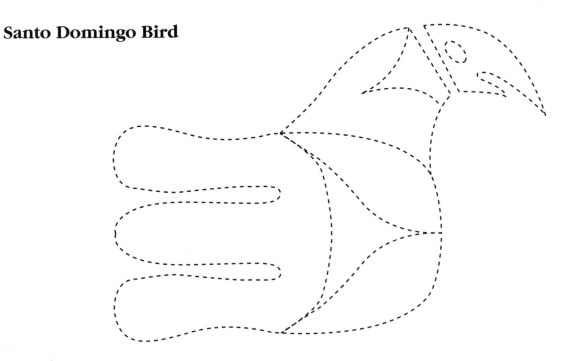

Hopi Pottery

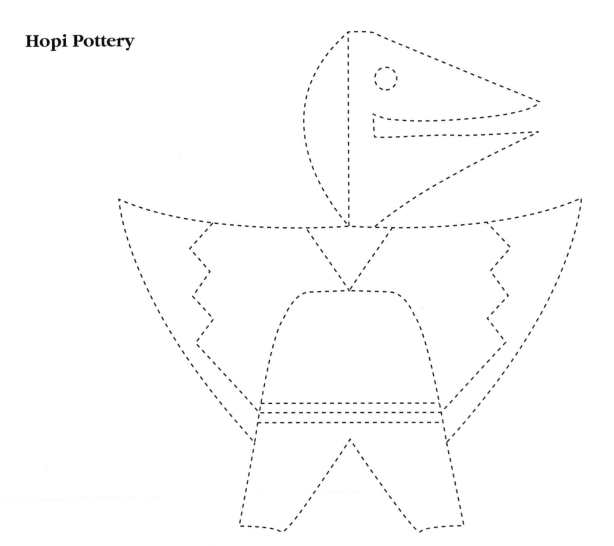

Native American Designs for Quilting – Dr. Joyce Mori

Northwest Coast Weaving

Hopi Basket

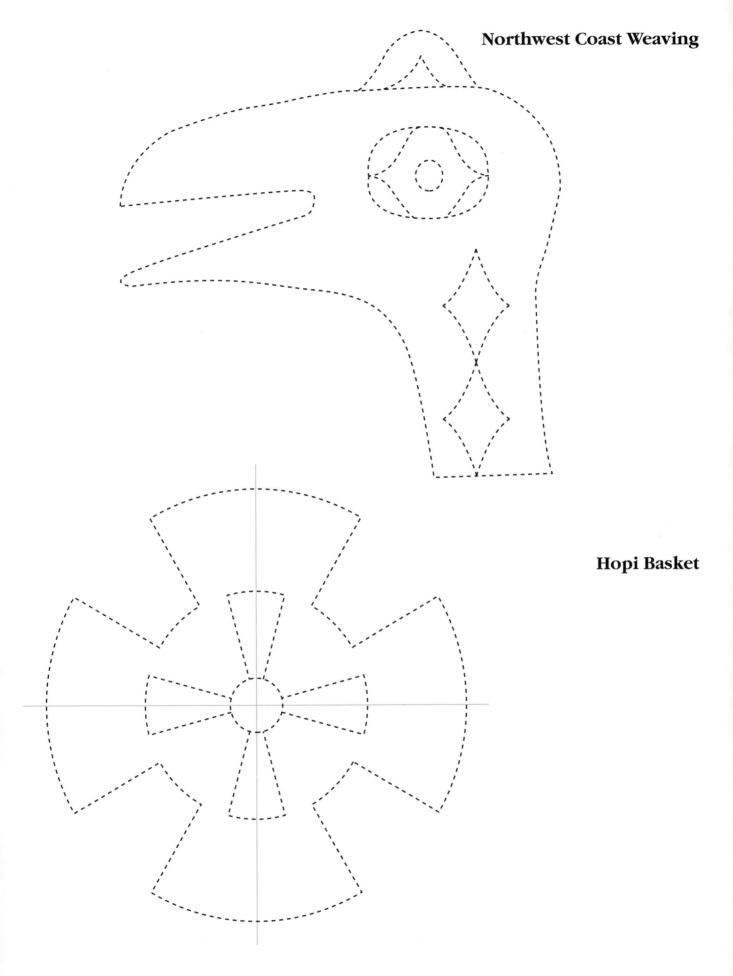

Pawnee Design

Navajo Weaving

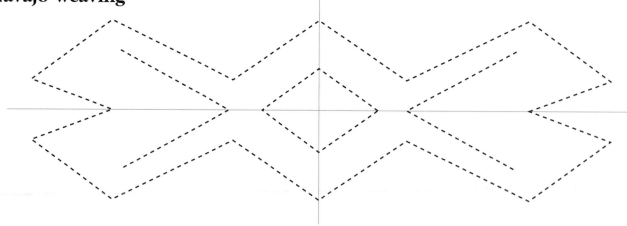

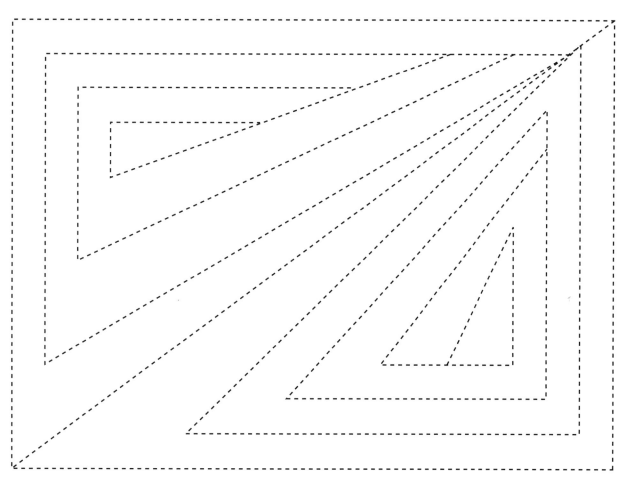

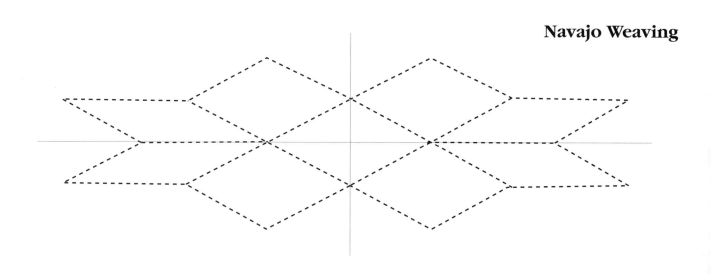

Prehistoric Southwest Pottery

Native American Designs for Quilting – Dr. Joyce Mori

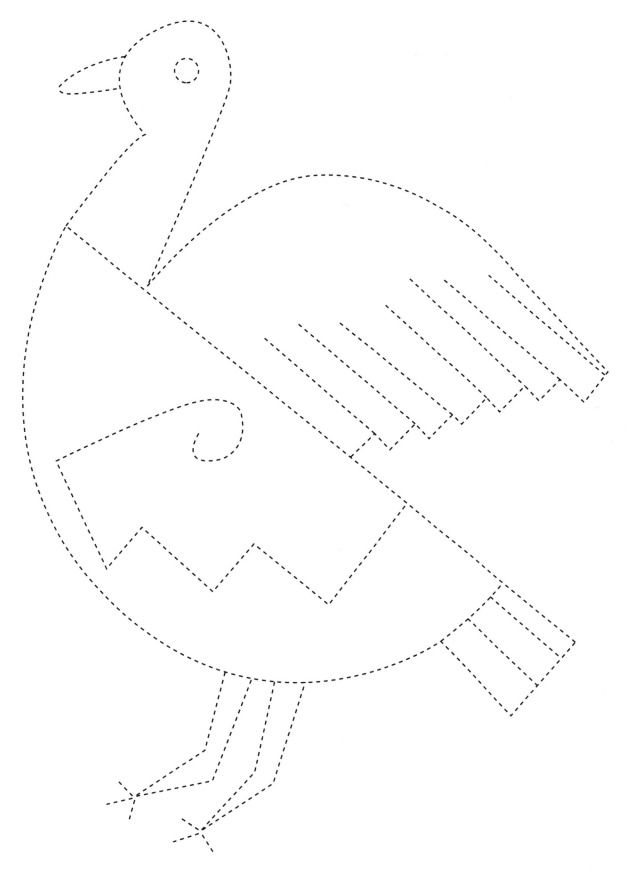

Southwest Pottery

Northwest Coast Weaving

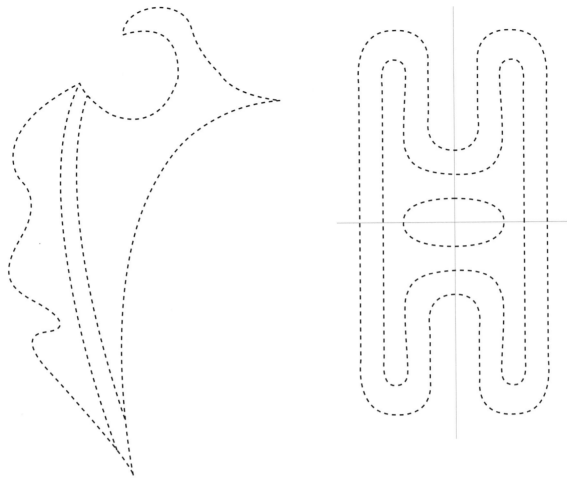

Prehistoric Southwest Blanket

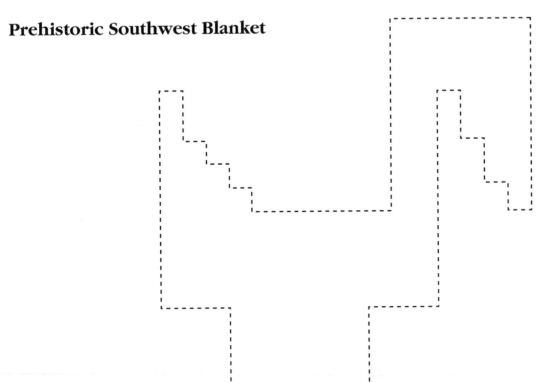

Native American Designs for Quilting – Dr. Joyce Mori

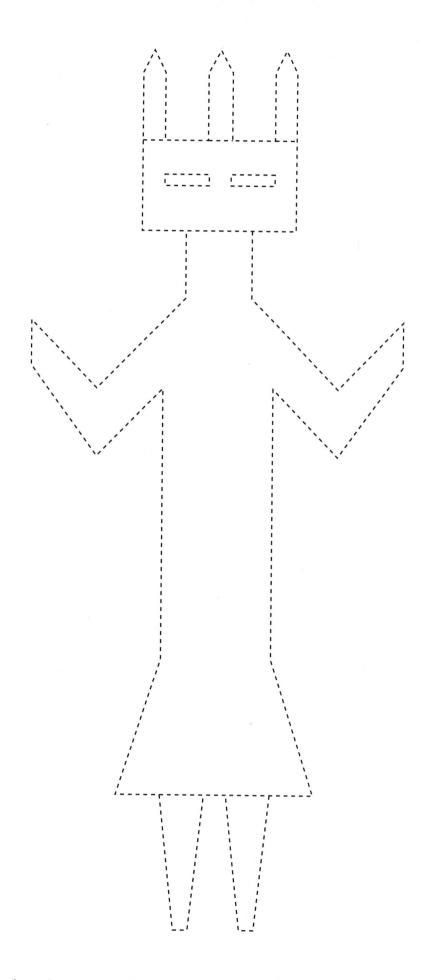

More Motifs and Designs

I feel strongly that many Native American designs, and in fact designs from all cultures, are suitable for all types of quilts and not just those with a specific ethnic theme. This section of the book includes a wide range of motifs – geometric, floral, and abstract – that can be used alone, combined with other motifs, or manipulated as suggested previously.

Let your creativity soar as you look at the designs in this section. Challenge yourself to use these designs to create new designs. Once you start manipulating and creating new quilting patterns, you will quickly find it is another enjoyable aspect of the entire quiltmaking process.

Zia Pottery

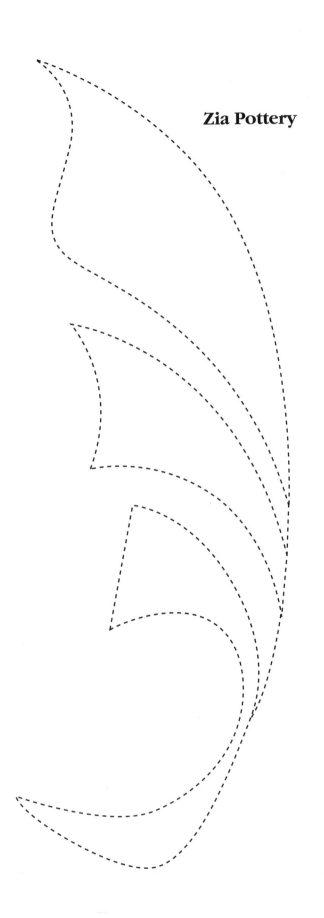

Zia Pottery

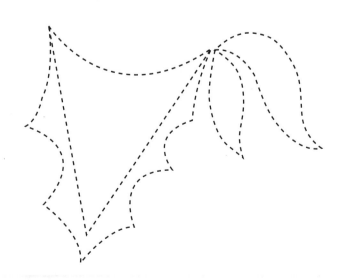

Southwest Pottery

Southwest Jewelry

Navajo Basket

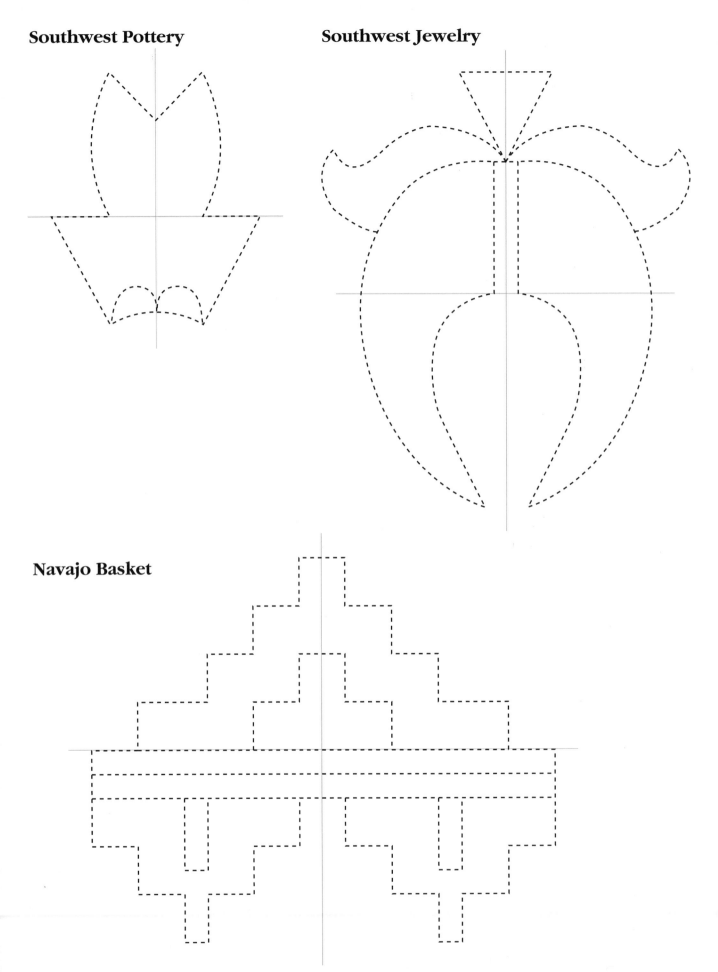

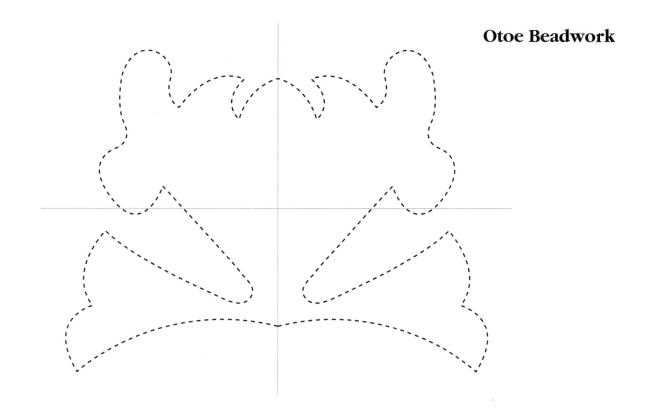

Hopi Pottery

Southwest Pottery

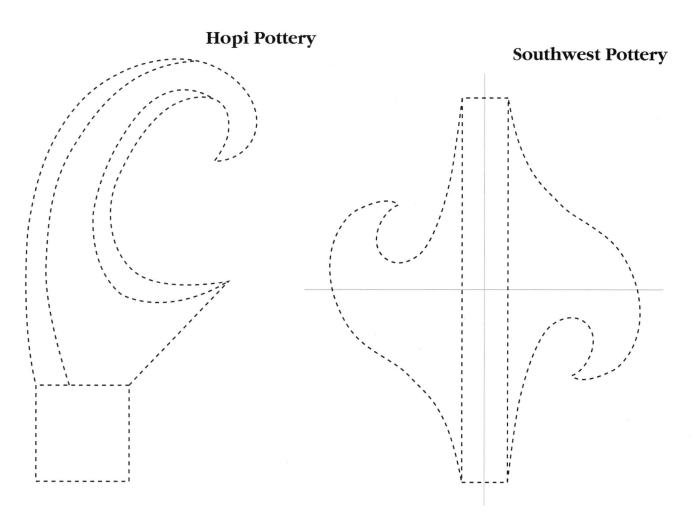

Plateau Quillwork

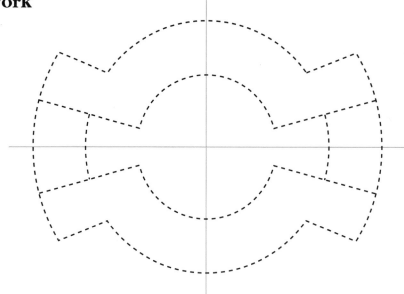

Prehistoric Southwest Pottery

Nez Perce Beadwork

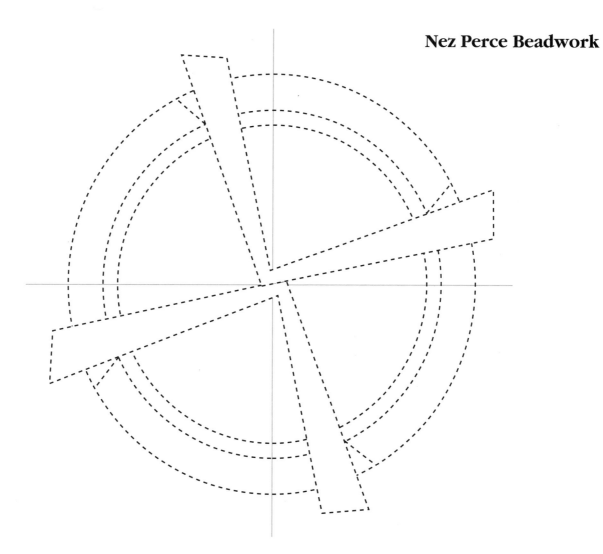

Southwest Basketry

Hopi Pottery

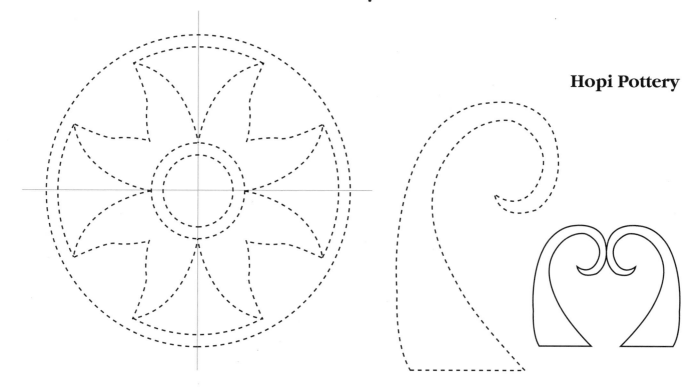

Hopi Pottery

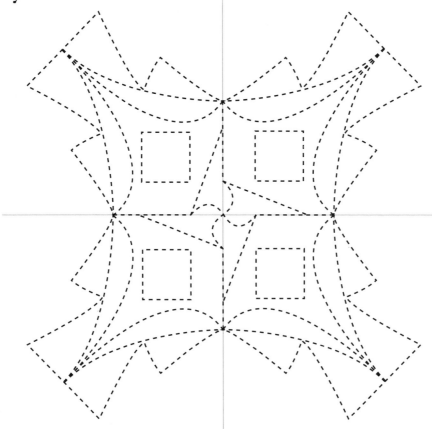

Hopi Pottery

Native American Designs for Quilting – Dr. Joyce Mori

Osage Beadwork

Southwest Pottery

Woodland Beadwork

Navajo Rug

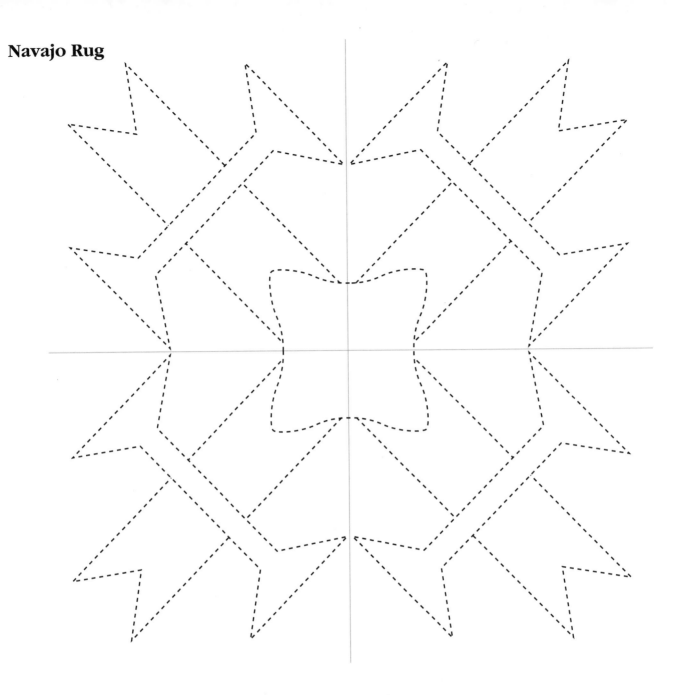

Sikyatki (Prehistoric) Southwest Pottery

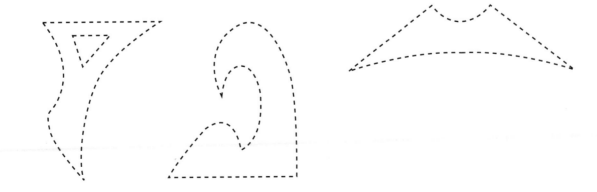

Native American Designs for Quilting – Dr. Joyce Mori

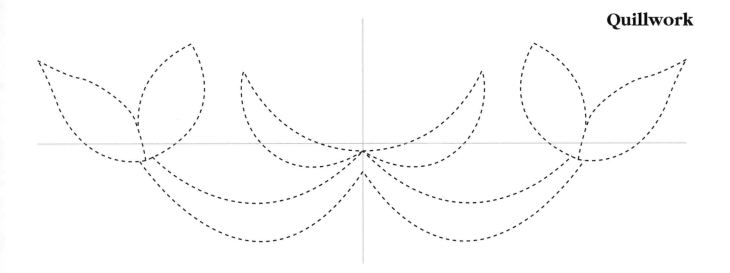

Southwest Pottery

Southwest Pottery

Southwest Pottery

Sioux Quillwork

Southwest Pottery

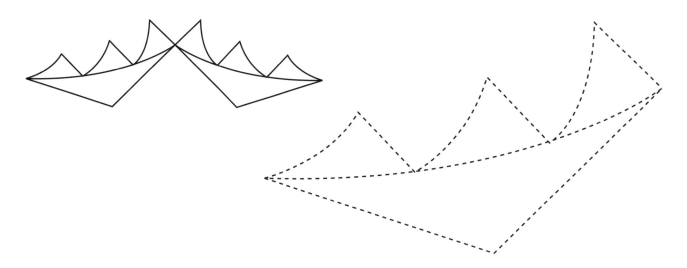

San Ildefonso Pottery

Southwest Pottery

Micmac Pipe

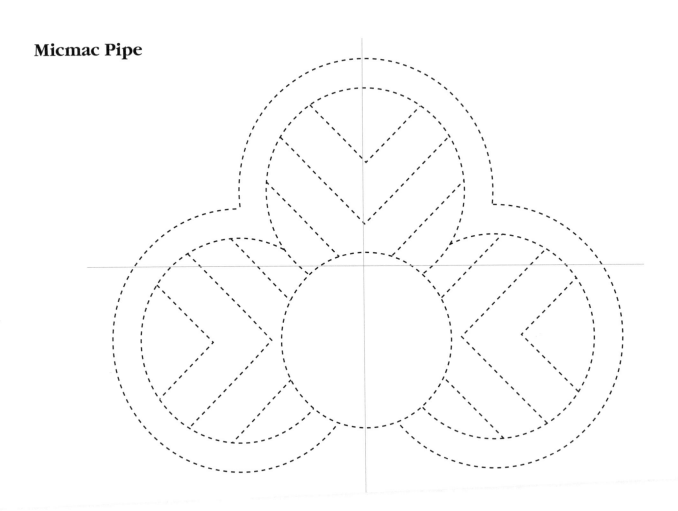

Hopi Wicker Plaque

Native American Designs for Quilting – Dr. Joyce Mori

Northeast Woodland Beadwork

Southwest Pottery

Acoma Pottery

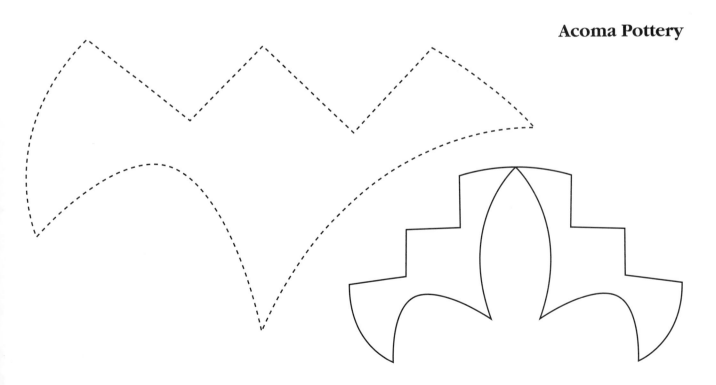

Tlingit Basket

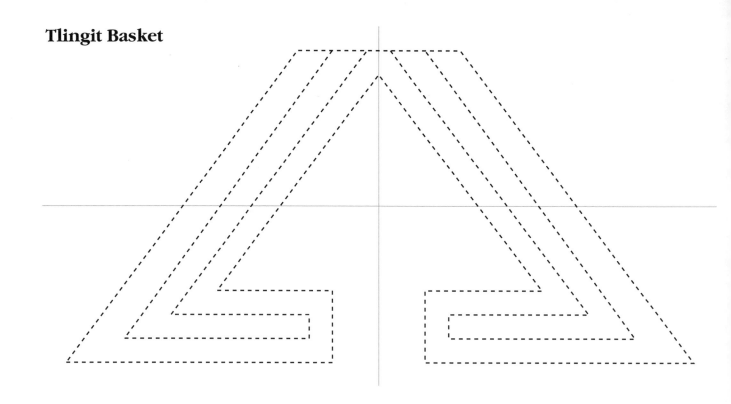

Hupa Basket

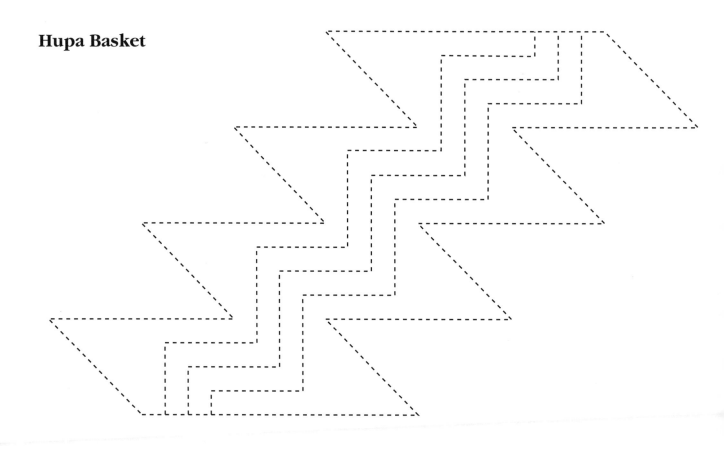

Native American Designs for Quilting – Dr. Joyce Mori

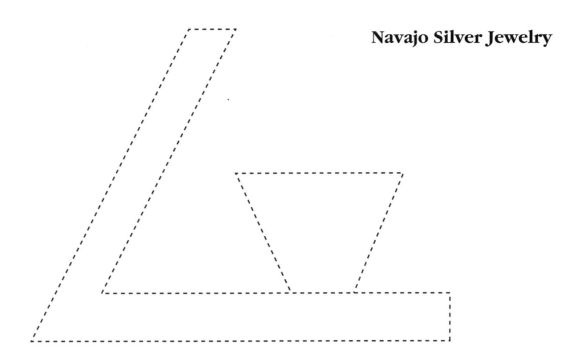

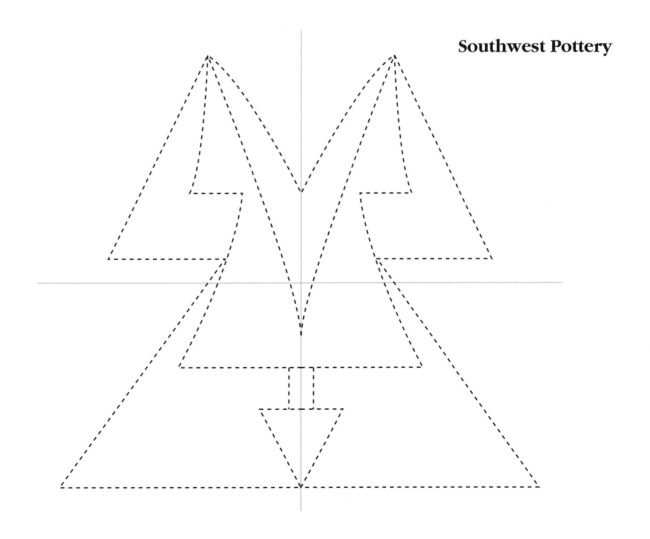

Ojibwa Beadwork

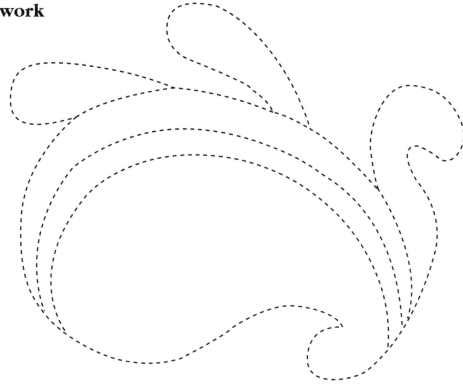

Southwest Silverwork

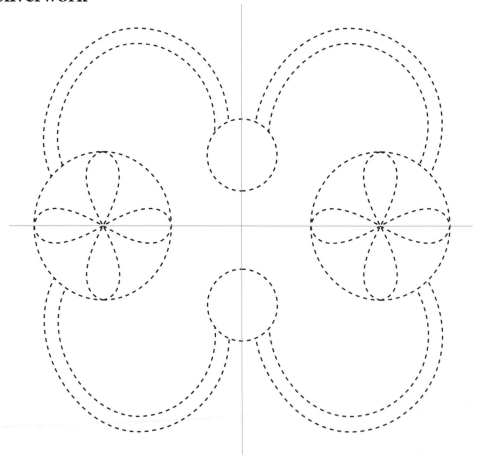

Native American Designs for Quilting – Dr. Joyce Mori

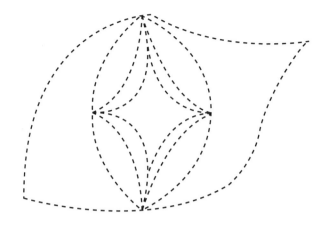

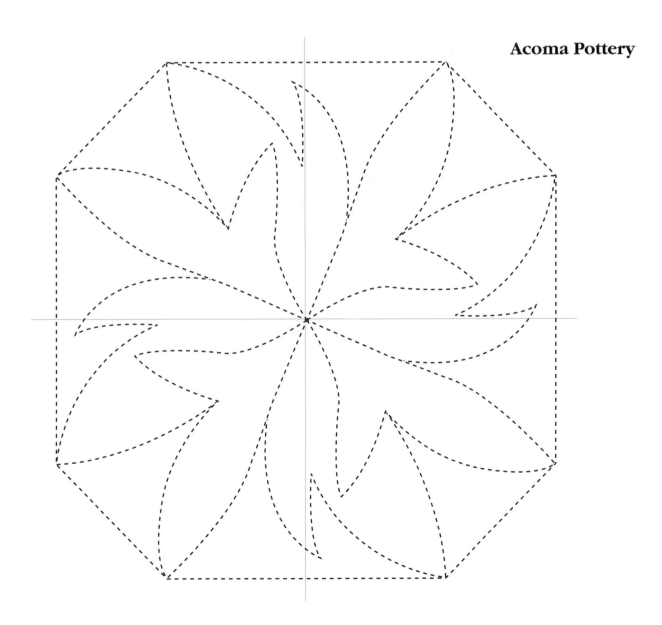

Northwest Beadwork

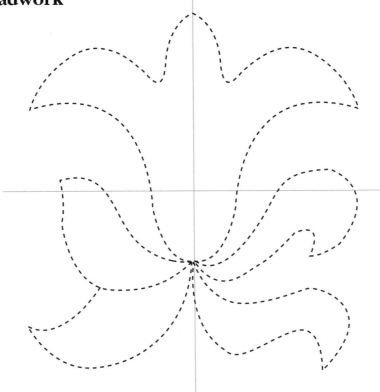

Southwest Silverwork

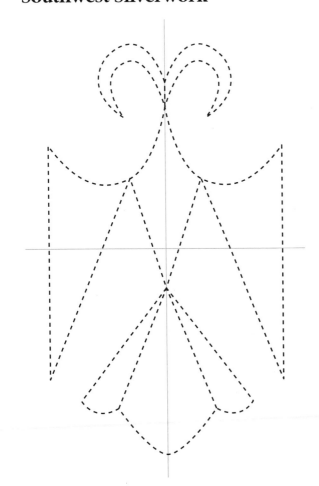

Southwest Pottery

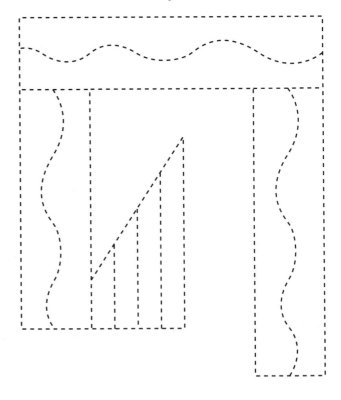

Native American Designs for Quilting – Dr. Joyce Mori

OTHER GREAT BOOKS BY DR. JOYCE MORI

Celebrate our Native American heritage with unique and bold designs found throughout Dr. Joyce Mori's series of pattern books.

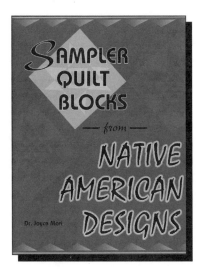

Sampler Quilt Blocks from Native American Designs

Explores designs adapted from cornhusk bags! Over 30 pieced block and border designs help create beautiful quilts that express the Native American heritage.
80 pgs, 8½" x 11", #4512 (ISBN: 0-89145-847-6)
$14.95

Quilting Patterns from Native American Designs

Presented as ready-to-use quilting patterns, these designs originated from pottery, rugs, and silverwork items. Each geometric design, stylized plant and animal, or graceful swirl promotes cultural awareness and spans a wide time frame, from prehistoric to recent time.
80 pgs., 8½" x 11", #3467 (ISBN: 0-89145-813-1)
$12.95

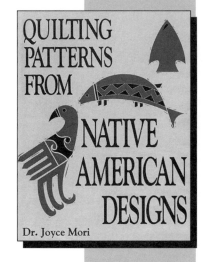

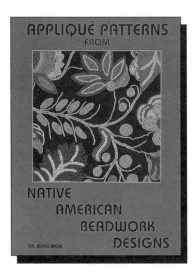

Appliqué Patterns from Native American Beadwork Designs

Native American beadwork provides an exciting source of inspiration for appliqué designs. This book presents full-size patterns and instructions for 10 floral projects.
96 pgs., 9" x 12", #3790 (ISBN: 0-89145-826-3)
$14.95

Available at local quilt, fabric, and book stores, or order direct.

ORDER TOLL-FREE: 7:00 am–5:00 pm CST
1 - 8 0 0 - 6 2 6- 5 4 2 0

American Quilter's Society

P. O. Box 3290 • Paducah, KY 42002-3290
FAX 502-898-8890 *http://www.AQSquilt.com*

For a complete listing of AQS titles, write or call the American Quilter's Society.